D0323749

EVALUATION IN LEGISLATION

Volume 5
Sage Research Progress Series in Evaluation

SAGE RESEARCH PROGRESS SERIES IN EVALUATION

The Series Editors and the Publishers are grateful to those Board members who refereed this year's volumes.

SAGE RESEARCH PROGRESS SERIES IN EVALUATION
Volume 5

Edited by
FRANKLIN M. ZWEIG

EVALUATION
IN
LEGISLATION

Foreword by
SENATOR HARRISON A. WILLIAMS, JR.

Published in cooperation with the
EVALUATION RESEARCH SOCIETY

SAGE PUBLICATIONS   Beverly Hills   London

For information address:

SAGE Publications, Inc.
275 South Beverly Drive
Beverly Hills, California 90212

SAGE Publications Ltd
28 Banner Street
London EC1Y 8QE, England

Printed in the United States of America

Library of Congress Cataloging in Publication Data
Main entry under title:

Evaluation in legislation.

    (Sage research progress series in evaluation ; v. 5)
    "Published in cooperation with the Evaluation
Research Society."
    1. Evaluation research (Social action programs)—
United States. 2. Policy sciences. 3. United States.
Congress. 4. Legislation—United States. I. Zweig,
Franklin M. II. Evaluation Research Society.
III. Series.
H62.5.U5E88   309.1'07'232   79-21968
ISBN 0-8039-1387-7
ISBN 0-8039-1388-5 pbk.

FIRST PRINTING

Contents

ABOUT THIS SERIES

The SAGE RESEARCH PROGRESS SERIES IN EVALUATION is a series of concisely edited works designed to present notable, previously unpublished writing on topics of current concern to the evaluation community. In keeping with a vision of evaluation as a methodological enterprise with outcomes at both the policy-making and services delivery levels, the series is designed to present state-of-the-art volumes for use by instructors and students of evaluation, researchers, practitioners, policy-makers, and program administrators.

Each volume (4 to 6 new titles will be published in each calendar year) focuses on themes which emerge from the previous year's annual meeting of the Evaluation Research Society—revised and supplemented by specially commissioned works.

The series begins in 1979 with five volumes, largely selected from papers delivered at the 2nd Annual Meeting of the Evaluation Research Society held in Washington, D.C. on November 2-4, 1978. The volumes in this inaugural year include:

QUALITATIVE AND QUANTITATIVE METHODS IN EVALUATION RESEARCH, edited by Thomas D. Cook and Charles S. Reichardt

EVALUATOR INTERVENTIONS: Pros and Cons, edited by Robert Perloff

TRANSLATING EVALUATION INTO POLICY, edited by Robert F. Rich

THE EVALUATOR AND MANAGEMENT, edited by Herbert C. Schulberg and Jeanette M. Jerrell

EVALUATION IN LEGISLATION, edited by Franklin M. Zweig

We are pleased that these initial volumes in the *SAGE RESEARCH PROGRESS SERIES IN EVALUATION* so well represent significant interdisciplinary contributions to the literature. Comments and suggestions from our readers will be welcomed.

SERIES EDITORS:

Susan E. Salasin, National Institute of Mental Health
Robert Perloff, University of Pittsburgh

The Honorable Harrison A. Williams, Jr.

Chairman
Committee on Labor and Human Resources
U.S. Senate

FOREWORD

During the past year, the jurisdiction of the Committee on Labor and Human Resources included nearly 2,000 federal programs carried out by the Departments of Labor and Health, Education and Welfare and 17 independent agencies, totaling over $50 billion in federal expenditures. These programs touched the lives of virtually all Americans, young and old, rich and poor, male and female, persons of all colors, creeds, and ethnic backgrounds.

These programs were built into a labor and human services structure over a 50-year period. They provide the bulwark of federal efforts in elementary and secondary education, employment, health services, programs for older Americans, services to handicapped persons, alcohol and drug abuse prevention and treatment, arts and humanities programs, higher education and child and human development programs, among others. They are the legacy of the great outpouring of American hope embodied in such landmark legislation as the G.I. Bill, the Land Grant Colleges Act, the Economic Opportunity Act, the Education of All Handicapped Children Act, the Civil Rights Act of 1964, the Older Americans Act of 1965, the Community Mental Health Centers Act, and Food and Drug Act, and the Employee Retirement Income Security Act.

The emergence and maturation of the applied social sciences accompanied that profound legislative development. These disciplines provided the foundation of a guidance system for improving and renovating the various programs authorized by social legislation. Program evaluation emerged as a young and hopeful focus for implementation of that social science guidance system. Program evaluation tools were vastly improved during the decade of the 1970s. In the same era, constant dollar support for many social programs declined along with public perceptions of their adequacy. Once universally supported, these programs in 1979 face a constituency of doubters. Economic swings—recessions and gouging inflation—and the persistence of debiliating social problems have taken their toll on the confidence of citizens and policymakers alike. Indeed, one former Congressman on the occasion of his retirement recently remarked, "Politics has gone from the age of 'Camelot' when all things were possible to the age of 'Watergate' when all things are suspect."

Against this background, evaluation is more than ever needed in legislative activity. More than any time in memory, elected representatives must be able to argue from a factual base, sometimes in light of awesome technicalities. Congressional committees, for example, weigh enormous volumes of conflicting evidence in deciding whether to enact or extend programs and benefits. Evaluation holds promise of systematically and sensibly locating, collecting, analyzing, and interpreting the needed evidence. Yet the promise of program evaluation remains unfulfilled, because we do not yet have the continuous information flow from evaluators essential to make policy and programmatic decisions of immense importance.

I hope that this brief volume will constitute one small, yet significant step in sophisticating evaluation for use in Congress and in the other legislatures of the nation. Its sources spring in large part from the committee which I am privileged to chair. The editor has served on my staff in various capacities since 1973. Many of the contributing authors have had connections with the work of the Committee on Labor and Human Resources, either in their capacities within various congressional agencies or by virtue of their help as expert witnesses.

Roots of a personal nature have spurred my own interest in evaluation and its relationship to legislation as well. Jeanette Williams and Marcia Guttentag, in connection with committee staff, proposed in 1977 that the committee convene the first congressional hearing on the cost, management and utilization of program evaluation. The subsequent hearing set the stage for an extensive series of comprehensive policy oversight hearings: American Women and Human Resources Policy, The Workplace and Higher Education, Youth and the Workplace, the Human Side of the Nation's Urban Policy, Remedies to the Fragmentation of Human Services, and the Technology of Service Delivery.

Marcia's friendship and wise counsel established a foundation for our pursuit of these analyses of public policy and for elaboration of countless ideas for improving services to families. Her influence continues, in part through this volume.

I am pleased to introduce this book. It is a fitting invitation to professional evaluators to consider the legislatures of this nation as a welcoming client for their ideals and endeavors.

Washington, D.C.
August 1979

PREFACE

This book is a collection of original articles embracing evaluation, legislation, and public policy. It is a first attempt to probe a relationship between the legislative process and evaluative research as a tool available for use in the execution of that process.

The term *to probe a relationship* has been chosen purposefully. It is not clear as this volume is constructed that a pattern of transactions characteristic of a relationship currently exists between American legislatures and the institutions engaged in the conduct of evaluative research.

We have anecdotal evidence from recent experience that the Congress of the United States, our national legislature, has enlarged its managerial orientation as oversight activities and other budget-minded actions have replaced new, large-scale legislative initiatives. In Chapter 1 of this collection, Ronald Lee Hicks describes a signal aspect of this orientation as it has become embodied in recent proposals to enact a federal sunset act. Among its many other provisions for changing the legislative process, the sunset act would mandate Congress's systematic utilization of evaluative research. Sunset legislation was proposed incident to original proposals for a congressional budget act in the early 1970s. In spite of an 87-to-1 favorable vote by the Senate in the waning days of the 95th Congress, a sunset provision has not yet been enacted by both houses of Congress. Until that enactment, it will not be possible to do more than mine the rich veins of speculation as to a sunset measure's impact in bringing law-making and evaluative research closer together.

Hicks is Senior Analyst with the Senate Committee on Rules and Administration and is in the best possible position to describe and comment upon congressional efforts to consider sunset legislation. He chaired a year-long task force representing 25 chairmen of Senate committees to draft sunset legislation. The task force was charged by Senator Howard W. Cannon, then chairman of the rules committee, to evaluate all approaches to automatic program termination and evaluation and to recommend to the committee a measure which tapped the strengths of several formerly competing measures. Much of the task force's work was incorporated into S.2, the Sunset Act of 1978, a bill authored by Senator Edmund S. Muskie and 55 cosponsors which passed the Senate overwhelmingly in 1978.

Hicks's perspectives about sunset legislation are grounded in his experience. His prescriptions for evaluator action to make evaluative research more comprehensible within the ambit of the legislative process stem from his first-hand knowledge. If Congress establishes a sunset process in its effort to perfect reforms begun in the Budget Act, institutions and individuals conducting evaluation will draw upon Hicks's observations continuously.

The Budget Act, however, has been enacted and in fact has guided congressional activity during the second half of this decade. Widely regarded as successful in linking budget priorities to legislative actions, the Budget Act is considered the pivotal aspect of Congress's direct management of increasingly scarce governmental resources. Hillel Weinberg, in Chapter 2, explores the use of evaluative information in the conduct of the budget process. While Weinberg utilizes "policy analysis" as the organizing principle of his article, he frankly defines that principle as "empirical, explicit prospective or retrospective information on the effects of programs," a definition closely akin to that used by many experts to define evaluation. Weinberg approaches his subject from the dual vantage point of congressional staffer—he currently is legislative assistant to Congressman Benjamin A. Gilman (R-NY)—and as a Yale doctoral student in political science whose doctoral dissertation concerns the utilization of program evaluation by congressional committees.

The Budget Act created a modest evaluation market with Title VII and VIII of the act stimulating evaluation production among congressional agencies. As a consequence, the General Accounting Office (GAO) established its Program Analysis Division, one branch of which devotes its work exclusively to evaluative research. The division has spent several years in devising an appropriate strategy for congressional approaches to evaluative research. The task has not been an easy one. Difficulties faced by the division stemmed not only from considerable skepticism of evaluative research within the Congress but also the rapidly evolving foundation of evaluative research practice provided few fixed reference points upon which to anchor GAO's efforts. Titles VII and VIII of the Budget Act, it should be remembered, are largely permissive and lack the obligatory evaluation mandate upon which the Sunset Act is predicated. It is not surprising that the GAO has emphasized utilization of evaluation by the Congress as contrasted with production of that research.

Keith Marvin, Associate Director of GAO's Program Analysis Division, discusses in Chapter 3 his agency's current approach to evaluating the thousands of Federal programs supported by federal expenditures exceeding half a trillion dollars annually. Marvin's emphasis may stimulate controversy; his legislative emphasis upon utilization is nearly coterminous with the managerial emphasis embraced by the President's Office of Management and Budget. That emphasis holds that the purpose of evaluation is to improve the management of government service delivery. This approach seems implicitly to pinpoint the bureaucrat as the primary consumer of evaluative research and raises an issue: Can such an approach satisfy policymakers' requirements in determining policy desirability and salience as well as program delivery feasibility? Marvin is cautiously optimistic that both evaluative research audiences can be accommodated.

Marvin's colleagues at GAO, Carlotta Young and Joseph Comtois, provide a complementary view of evaluation utilization in Chapter 4. They structure questions deemed essential to congressional utilization of such research, array these questions as criteria for effective utilization, and provide a literature base within each criterion. The effect of the Young and Comtois article is to create a provisional stencil for replicating evaluative studies of use to Congress wherein a literature survey supports the authors' argument. That argument is tentative, however, reflecting the early stage of evaluation in legislation.

New and developing fields of endeavor require extensive effort in paradigm construction. Development of evaluative research in the legislative sphere is no exception as is well illustrated by Joseph Coates and Charles McClintock, authors of Chapters 5 and 6, respectively.

Coates tackles one of the most challenging issues confronting a managerially minded Congress—the construction of impact statements to accompany legislation. Coates's paradigm concerns Senate Rule 29.5, a requirement adopted in 1977 that all legislation favorably reported from Senate committees for action by the Senate body be accompanied by statements assessing the regulatory impact of such recommended legislation. Amid recent dissatisfaction with the extent to which Rule 29.5 has effectively been implemented since its adoption, Coates and coworkers at the

Congress's Office of Technology Assessment recently completed for Senator Harrison A. Williams, Jr., chairman of the Senate Committee on Labor and Human Resources, an exploratory paper entitled "Anticipating the Impacts of Legislation." The paper was distributed to all Senate Committees as an aid to predicting, locating, collecting, and synthesizing the retrospective information necessary to construct impact statements.

Is Coates's work "evaluation"? It is in the global and heuristic sense in which the term is used legislatively, but it contains a special feature: Anticipating legislative impact requires a prospective (as opposed to retrospective) orientation and the employment of forecasting (as opposed to net outcome) methodologies.

McClintock's analysis may equally be described as a paradigm—a model for ordering evaluative information in the legislative arena. McClintock's subject is also the Senate committee, but his work is focused upon the possible linkages between budget information and other sources of program review data in the committee process. Concerned with the application of evaluative research techniques in his capacity as a professor at Cornell University's College of Human Ecology, McClintock draws extensively upon his experience as a contract consultant to the Senate Committee on Labor and Human Resources in 1978. During that year, the Labor and Human Resources Committee developed a program review system. McClintock uses the orderly and logical approach of survey research in prescribing an information-based, budget-related program review mechanism for committee use.

Eleanor Chelimsky, author of Chapter 7, critiques the strengths and weaknesses of governmentally sponsored, broad-aim demonstration programs as an evaluative device of value to legislative activity.

Chelimsky is Director of Policy Analysis for the Metrek Division of MITRE Corporation, the nation's largest nonprofit contractor of analytic and experimental services to the federal government. She is no stranger to the evaluation of congressionally originated, broad-scale, demonstration projects having had important roles in MITRE's assessment of several such efforts. Chelimsky's view is that demonstration programs are often ineffective, yet increasingly relied upon by the Congress as a means to evaluate policy alternatives. In the absence of agreed-upon policy choices and in a time of economic austerity, Chelimsky contends, demonstration projects will find increasing favor in Congress. Convinced of the intractability of this trend, Chelimsky sets her sights upon improving the evaluative component of broad-aim demonstration programs. Some of her conclusions may prove controversial among evaluators. For example, Chelimsky recommends deployment of mixed evaluative strategies in every demonstration program. Chelimsky's support for carefully linked evaluation methodologies in such programs, however, will be well received by policy makers.

My essay, "The Evaluation Worldview of Congressional Staff," the last chapter of this collection, emerged in part from my own experience as staff counsel to the Senate Committee on Labor and Human Resources and in part from a workshop I was privileged to conduct for the 1978 meeting of the Evaluation Research Society.

The main theme of the essay is that the clash of morally armored constituencies in the legislative process produces a demand for evaluation as a means to perfect compromise among those constituencies' competing claims. This climate of continuing conflict, in my experience, comprises the context for congressional staff's perception of all aspects of evaluation.

The Evaluation Research Society workshop conducted in November 1978 was entitled "Legislative Process for Evaluators." It was predicated upon the notion that elected officials and their professional staff constitute an important client pool for evaluators having interests in public policy. Early in the course of the workshop, it became clear that the participating expert evaluators had difficulties in anticipating legislative client response, in large measure due to lack of familiarity with the culture of the legislature, particularly the conflict-shaped perceptions of evaluation often held by congressional staff.

This final chapter, then, is meant to identify for evaluators some of the dynamics affecting congressional staff. Since staff increasingly are relied upon by elected legislators for carrying out research and for critiquing evaluation, and since the congressional committee system is where such activity is concentrated, I hope that this chapter may prove useful to professional evaluators.

I am indebted to the authors of the original articles comprising this volume. Their commitment to exploring this new, largely uncharted subject made the book possible. It is the hope of all of us that this volume will make a small contribution upon which later work can be built.

I wish to express my gratitude as well to several additional persons who have encouraged this collection.

Senator Harrison A. Williams, Jr., chairman of the Senate Committee on Labor and Human Resources, has been unstinting in his support of program evaluation refinement for legislative purposes. His vision and commitment to improved social policy have buoyed prospects for evaluation in legislation and are reflected by the extensive hearing he chaired late in 1977 on the cost, management, and utilization of program evaluation. Senator Williams's perspective is well presented in his generous Foreword to this volume, for which I am most grateful.

I am deeply indebted to Jeanette Williams for constant support and encouragement. Her advocacy of evaluation in social policy development has spurred her colleagues to explore new frontiers and technologies in aid of the people of the United States who view the Committee on Labor and Human Resources as their forum for national legislation. As chair of the advisory committee of the stress and families project of the National Institute of Mental Health, Jeanette has guided a working merger between policy formulation and evaluative research. The perspective emanating from that merger provides continuous inspiration for those of us working with her.

Stephen J. Paradise, Staff Director of the Committee on Labor and Human Resources, has provided constant help and encouragement. His continuing interest in the development of evaluation's relationship to legislation has been indispensable to the committee's pursuit of it. His review and critique have been most valuable to me.

The Evaluation Research Society has continuously supported efforts to relate legislation, policy making, and evaluation. Ms. Susan Salasin, the editor of this series of volumes, has assisted me throughout. Her talented and thoughtful insights are very much appreciated. Dr. Lois-Ellen Datta, President of the society, has carried forward the society's commitment to viewing evaluation as a tool for constructive change and improvement and has ably continued this posture initiated under the society's initial Presidential leadership, Dr. Marcia Guttentag and Dr. Robert Perloff.

Marcia Guttentag was a good friend—personally and professionally. She is missed. I am certain that she would approve our endeavors and urge on our initial work in this area. Bob Perloff has admirably implemented directions first initiated under Marcia's tenure as the society's president and has made unique contributions to linking evaluation and legislation through his counsel and vision.

President of Sage Publications, Sara Miller McCune has been patient, encouraging, and always helpful. It is a tribute to her as well that this series has been brought into existence. It is a timely series and marks a needed step in the orderly advance of evaluation as a professional area of competence and authority.

Finally, many thanks go Ms. Julie Kolberg who typed part of this manuscript and made helpful suggestions for its improvement.

The views expressed by the contributors to this volume are their own opinions and do not reflect the opinions or positions of any legislative entity or agency of government.

Franklin M. Zweig
Washington, D.C.
July 1979

Ronald Lee Hicks

*U.S. Senate Committee on Rules
and Administration*

1

SUNSET LEGISLATION

These remarks are in the nature of suggestions to the evaluation community regarding the provision of effective support to the Congress under a Federal "sunset" procedure. As such, the remarks are based on four presuppositions: (1) that a Federal sunset bill will eventually be enacted; (2) that one of the purposes of such a bill is to increase the use of systematic program evaluation by the Congress in judging policies and programs; (3) that there is a role for professional evaluators to play in this process; and (4) that the success of the venture will depend partly on the degree to which evaluations are relevant to and useful in the legislative process.

These comments focus mainly upon a significant provision of S.2, the Sunset Act of 1979, a bill introduced in the Senate in the 95th and 96th Congresses by Senator Edmund S. Muskie (D-Maine) with over half of the Senate as cosponsors.[1] The focal provision is the requirement contained in Title III that congressional committees select a few programs each Congress for in-depth reexamination. Title III appears to be the provision which will most closely and directly involve the evaluation community in the legislative process.

Two other provisions of S.2 could intensify evaluator-legislator interactions as well. Title I requires that all programs be reauthorized every 10 years, according to a schedule set forth in the bill, and prescribes that reauthorizations be preceded by standardized committee reviews of the programs; Title II mandates the establishment and maintenance of an inventory of Federal programs.[2]

Congressional interest in program reexaminations is greater now than at any time in recent memory. This interest is reflected not only in the various

---

AUTHOR'S NOTE: *The views expressed are those of the author and not necessarily those of the Committee on Rules and Administration or any member thereof.*

titles of S.2, the Sunset Act of 1979, but also is evident in various regulatory reform and legislative veto proposals now pending in Congress. This interest seems to be underpinned by a number of commonly held perceptions:

(1) Room must be found within present budget ceilings for new initiatives, instead of through growth in aggregate spending, increased taxation, or enlarged budgetary deficits.

(2) Programs enacted in the past few decades are not working as well as was intended.

(3) Regulatory activity is increasingly unnecessary or dysfunctional.

(4) Rational evaluation will facilitate better (more fair, more consistent, more effective) public policy than other approaches to reducing spending, such as formula ceilings or across-the-board percentage cuts of appropriations.

SUNSET REEXAMINATION OF FEDERAL PROGRAMS

Not all programs are currently covered by the periodic reauthorization of public laws and there is no standard reauthorization time period applicable to all programs. Furthermore, no standard is applicable to the form and content of congressional committees' recommendations in reporting legislation authorizing or reauthorizing programs.

Title I of S.2 seeks to overcome this absence of legislative standardization by establishing a 10-year schedule during which all Federal programs would be subject to automatic termination, review, and reauthorization according to the Federal subfunction in which they are classified.[3] Title I also establishes a minimum review standard, principally a committee determination as to whether a terminating program has fulfilled its legislative objectives. Program reexamination in the context of Title I is a global assessment of program effectiveness drawing upon secondary analysis of data accumulated from a potpourri of executive branch and non-Federal studies.[4]

Title II mandates the establishment and maintenance of an inventory of Federal programs, containing for each program the following information:

(1) the specific provision(s) of law authorizing the program

(2) the committees of the Senate and the House of Representatives which have legislative or oversight jurisdiction over the program

(3) a brief statement of the purpose(s) to be achieved by the program

(4) the committees which have jurisdiction over legislation providing new budget authority for the program, including the appropriate subcommittees of the Committees on Appropriations of the Senate and the House of Representatives

(5) the agency and, if applicable, the subdivision thereof responsible for administering the program

(6) the grants-in-aid, if any, provided by such program to state and local governments

(7) the next reauthorization date for the program

(8) a unique identification number which links the program and functional category structure

(9) the year in which the program was established and, when applicable, the year in which the program expires

(10) when applicable, the year in which new budget authority for the program was last authorized and the year in which current authorizations of new budget authority expire

(11) whether the new budget authority provided for such programs is: (a) authorized for a definite period of time; (b) authorized in a specific dollar amount but without limit of time; (c) authorized without limit of time or dollar amounts; (d) not specifically authorized; or (e) permanently provided

(12) the amounts of new budget authority authorized and provided for the program for each of the preceding four fiscal years and, when applicable, expected to be expended in each of the four succeeding fiscal years

(13) the functional and subfunctional category in which the program is presently classified and was classified under the fiscal year 1979 budget

(14) the identification code and title of the appropriation account in which budget authority is provided for the program.

Use of computer technology would facilitate production of special-purpose program lists from inventory data sorted on such criteria as date established, date last authorized, cost, and so on. While the primary purpose of the inventory is to support the processes established by Titles I and III, the establishment, maintenance, and publication of such an inventory would by itself stimulate a lot of program review. Information of this nature is simply not available currently.

Title III requires congressional committees to include in their annual funding resolutions for the first session of each Congress plans for reexamination of programs during that Congress, estimated completion date of such studies, and the estimated costs for each reexamination. In a report accompanying their yearly request for funds, committees are required to provide further information including a description of the planned reexamination and whether the reexamination will be conducted by the committee, by an executive agency, by a congressional agency, or by a nongovernmental organization under the committee's direction. Consideration of each committee's funding resolution is not in order if such information is lacking and if reports of completed program reexamination is lacking and if reports of completed program reexaminations scheduled for completion in the preceding Congress have not been submitted for printing. Title III is regarded as providing sufficient incentives for reexamination to be undertaken and completed while at the same time providing ample opportunities for the Senate and the House of Representatives to redirect committees' reexamination of priorities if they so choose by amendment of the committee's funding resolutions.

Flexibility in designing reexamination is essential given the many differences that exist among Federal programs. The most obvious differences are, of course, size and cost, but others are significant. Some are: (1) the extent of direct Federal action, as opposed to programs operated through the Federal subsidy by state, county, or city governments or by private institutions; (2) the degree to which the program is a central function of the Federal government, for example, national defense, and therefore unlikely to be discontinued; (3) the method of program administration, for example, tax incentives, grants and contracts, licensing, inspections and compliance enforcement; (4) the tangibility of the program goal or product, for example, ship construction as contrasted with cultural exchange programs with foreign countries; and (5) the degree to which there is actual or implied commitment to continuity, for example, social security payments as opposed to assistance in the preparation of tax returns. It seems likely that such differences would lead to a variety of evaluative approaches, some perhaps yet to be developed.

Title III reexamination guidelines should be a source of assistance for those members of the evaluation community who have been laboring in the area of improving legislative program review. The following are the proposed work products for Title III reviews:

(1) an identification of the objectives intended for the program and the problem it was intended to address

(2) an identification of any trends, developments, and emerging conditions which are likely to affect the future nature and extent of the problems or needs which the program is intended to address and an assessment of the potential primary and secondary effects of the proposed program

(3) an identification of any other program having potentially conflicting or duplicative objectives

(4) a statement of the number and types of beneficiaries or persons served by the program

(5) an assessment of the effectiveness of the program and the degrees to which the original objectives of the program or groups of programs have been achieved

(6) an assessment of the cost effectiveness of the program, including, when appropriate, a cost-benefit analysis of the operation of the program
(7) an assessment of the relative merits of alternative methods which could be considered to achieve the purposes of the program
(8) information on the regulatory, privacy, and paperwork impacts of the program.

Under Title III provisions, departments and agencies are required to submit reports of their own findings, recommendations, and justifications six months before the scheduled completion dates for committee reexamination reviews. While it might not seem obvious, the legislative language of much of the Sunset Act is intended to accommodate major reexaminations which span more than one Congress. This would be accomplished through timing (originally or by amendment) report dates to occur in a subsequent Congress and by continuous reference to the reexamination effort in subsequent funding resolutions.

The procedures further provide that the results of reexaminations are to be published as official documents. Under the current printing laws, this will result in approximately 2,000 copies being printed and distributed to executive departments and depository libraries, as well as the House and Senate document rooms from which they can be obtained by the press and the public. The purpose of publication is to ensure that the results of the reexaminations enter the arena of public discussion and thus contribute to the shaping of informed public opinion regarding the merits of programs.

LEGISLATIVE ENACTMENT AND JURISDICTION OF COMMITTEES

It goes without saying that the Federal government is responsible for an extensive number and a wide variety of programs. A work force of 2.8 million civilian employees carries out such varied missions as inspecting meat packing plants; keeping aircraft in the air at safe distances from each other; sending income checks to millions of retired or disabled citizens; providing tactile materials and audio devices to blind or visually impaired persons; prosecuting and defending criminal cases and civil litigation; rescuing persons lost at sea; building and operating instruments which carry out explorations on the moon and planets; ascertaining the timing and the nature of future events, such as economic, climatic, and geologic changes; and so on.

This extensive structure with its myriad responsibilities is administered by the President of the United States. Before programs can be administered, however, they must be authorized through legislation. Thus, the initial and final responsibility for what is and what is not to be public policy rests in the Congress. And it is a fundamental responsibility of Congress to know whether and to what extent the programs it has authorized are working and to make such modifications that are necessary or are desired by the people. The legislative process is inherently less orderly than the executive process. When a law has been passed and has become an administrative responsibility of the President, it represents a consensus that a particular thing should or should not be done. The essential and critical role of the Congress is to be the instrument, the process, the mechanism through which 230 million people reach a consensus on a matter of public policy. What the press and other spokesmen for specific courses of action often criticize as inaction on the part of the Congress is a manifestation that no broad public consensus exists for one course or another. An inherent requirement of a system of self-government is that no law should be enacted in the absence of a broad and enduring consensus, no matter how long that takes to achieve. Spokesmen for particular viewpoints are, of course, entitled to think that the proposals they advocate are superior and compelling, but one of the strengths of Congress as an institution is that particularistic views are forced to be reconciled with others before proposed programs find sufficient consensus to bring about their adoption as a matter of public policy.

In the drive to reach sufficient consensus, legislative committees are the principal instruments of Congress for the formulation and adoption of legislation. Committees draft bills and provide a forum for public critique by means of public hearings. Committees are the entities most centrally relevant to the initiation of new programs, the monitoring of their performance, and modification or termination of their activities. It is entirely appropriate therefore that Federal sunset proposals build on the existing process which authorizes legislation giving rise to and direction for public programs.

It might be useful to mention here some basic characteristics of Senate committees. First, there are 15 so-called "standing" committees and 5 special and select committees.[5] Of the 15 standing committees, 13 are known as authorizing committees[6] which simply means that they are the committees which authorize programs through enactment of laws. It is the legislation reported by these committees which vests authority in government entities to operate Federal programs.[7] The entire universe of the Federal government is distributed among congressional committees with authorizing jurisdiction. Jurisdiction is the power of a committee to act on subject matter for legislation. The jurisdiction of the Senate Committee on Agriculture, Nutrition, and Forestry, for example, reads as follows:

> Committee on Agriculture, Nutrition, and Forestry, to which committee shall be referred all proposed legislation, messages, petitions, memorials, and other matters relating primarily to the following subjects:
>
> (1) agricultural economics and research
> (2) agricultural extension services and experiment stations
> (3) agricultural production, marketing, and stabilization of prices
> (4) agriculture and agricultural commodities
> (5) animal industry and diseases
> (6) crop insurance and soil conservation
> (7) farm credit and farm security
> (8) food from fresh waters
> (9) food stamp programs
> (10) forestry and forest reserves and wilderness areas other than those created from the public domain
> (11) home economics
> (12) human nutrition
> (13) inspection of livestock, meat, and agricultural products
> (14) pests and pesticides
> (15) plant industry, soils, and agricultural engineering
> (16) rural development, rural electrification, and watersheds
> (17) school nutrition programs.
>
> Such committee shall also study and review, on a comprehensive basis, matters relating to food, nutrition, and hunger, both in the United States and in foreign countries, and rural affairs, and report thereon from time to time.[8]

Committee jurisdictions are not stated in terms of Federal agencies, specific pieces of previously passed legislation, appropriations accounts, or the Federal budgetary classification scheme. They are stated in a separate, formal, written structure, and used, among other things, for deciding to which committee a bill is to be referred and for confirmation hearings antecedent to advice and consent of the Senate regarding Presidential nominations.

Authorizing committees in the Senate range in size from about 9 to about 18 members. (House committees are usually larger, the House having more than four times the number of members as the Senate, but only a few more committees.) Senators have multiple committee assignments, being required to serve on at least two committees and permitted in some instances to serve on more.[9] Most Senators are members of at least six subcommittees. This sometimes poses scheduling problems when committees or subcommittees on which a Senator serves meet at the same time. There is no automatic rotation of committee members. Members develop expertise in the subjects attributed to their committees' jurisdictions. Chairmen and ranking minority members of most committees are elected by vote of the Senate at the beginning of each Congress, acting on the recommendations of the respective party conferences, which in turn take seniority on the committee into consideration.

Committees hire staff to assist their work. The sizes of committee staff vary even more than the sizes of the committees themselves. All standing committees have 6 professional and 6 clerical staff members provided by public law. These are referred to as statutory positions.[10] In addition, committees have so-called "investigative" staff provided by committee funding resolutions acted on at the beginning of each congressional session. Staff hired for "inquiries and investigations" vary greatly among committees. For example, the Committee on Veterans' Affairs has fewer than 25 staff, while the Committees on the Judiciary and Governmental Affairs have over 150 each. Unlike members, staff do not serve on multiple committees. The total committee staff in the Senate is about 1,300. This number may be compared with a modest-size single Federal agency, the Labor-Management Services Administration in the Department of Labor, which has more than 1,500 staff; with 2.8 million total civilian employment in the executive branch; and with 4.9 million combined civilian and military employment in the executive branch.

With staff vastly limited in number when contrasted with the executive agencies, congressional committees deploy their employees at every step of the legislative process. Such deployment includes program review and obviously carries with it heavy burdens. It is unlikely, therefore, that additional burdens signaled by sunset legislation could adequately be carried by the work force currently available to congressional committees. The guidelines proposed in Title III alone could easily absorb the time and energies of the current committee staff workforce. And Title I, with its mandatory review of each Federal government program every 10 years, could be even more demanding of staff attention than Title III's elective reexaminations.

It is not surprising, then, that sunset proposals include means to permit committee implementation of their procedures beyond utilization of currently employed staff. Such means include a modest number of additional new staff members, mandates for the execution of required studies by congressional and Federal agencies, and authorization of funds for committee contracting of program reviews and reexamination by non-Federal evaluation personnel and organizations.

Resistance to any but very modest increases in staff size, however, makes the contract mechanism a likely approach for bringing significant numbers of evaluators into sunset procedures. It, therefore, seems warranted to venture some prescriptions for most productive interaction with sunset activities. Accordingly, the tentative prescriptions suggested below presume that most evaluators engaged in the implementation of sunset legislation will interface committees from a noncongressional organizational base.

PRESCRIPTIONS FOR EVALUATORS

One compelling attribute of evaluators' congressional audience—the committee members and the senior committee staff—is the intense time pressure under which it functions. This group has no time for and little patience with material not relevant to specific issues. The following suggestions are offered to assist evaluators in dealing with time stressed congressional personnel.

First, be clear and consise. Technical conclusions must be put forward in such a way that most people can readily understand their meaning and significance. Make no mistake, this will be a difficult task if the phrases *most people, readily understand,* and *meaning and significance* are taken as literally as I mean them. If on the second page of a report congressional readers encounter deltas, lambdas, and p-hats, they will never get to the third page. In order to avoid distracting technicalities, I offer as a model or guide a typical feature story in the *Wall Street Journal*. Quantitative facts, reinforced and made "live" by ancedotes, are used to convey a central point in a short space. Of course, a major committee program review will have voluminous technical back-up material, much of it legitimately susceptible to publication. Clear presentation in the body of the report is still essential.

Second, relevance is mandatory. It is necessary to maintain a focus on the policy questions behind an evaluation. "Nice to know" information or impractical alternatives or recommendations will not be tolerated. It will be helpful to gain the perspective of the legislature regarding a program by conducting a study of its legislative history. This may be difficult for organizations which have long worked with executive agencies, and might be close to impossible for persons conducting reviews from within the executive agencies. The focus of an agency in its evaluation is and should be the efficient and effective administration of the law. The focus of the legislature is much broader, as broad as whether there should continue to be such a law or not.

Third, contact must be maintained. The evaluator must not allow separation or isolation for the staff person (and I stress the singular) who will be overseeing the evaluation study. The price of even inadvertent separation will likely be a product that is off the mark or overlooks some important factors. The evaluator's work may be found incomprehensible, irrelevant, impractical, or just not useful.

Fourth, keep the end in sight. The end is not the submission of the report. The crucible in which the evaluator's product will likely be tested is the floor of the Senate and the House of Representatives. Do not skimp treating all sides of an issue openly and thoroughly. Make the effort to hear opposing arguments and find ways to have them vigorously argued. Be prepared to change your mind. Proposed changes in a major program will affect interests which will find voices to assail the evaluator's results and credibility. Studies must be of high enough quality to bear the scrutiny which could come from interests that feel threatened by its conclusions.

Fifth, be professional. The objective of a sunset study is the meaningful improvement of a public policy. The goal transcends lesser considerations and can provide new and meaningful utilization of the evaluator's skills. Do not become disillusioned if the results of your best efforts are not the deciding factor. Clearly, major policy changes will continue to occur as a result of shifts in public support and not as the result of cost-benefit analysis. Evaluation, however, properly utilized, can provide constructive influence.

CONCLUSIONS

The proposal for sunset legislation has been through three years of refinement and seems more broadly acceptable than when it was first introduced. While the idea of sunset seems to have been a major innovation in state government, periodic program reauthorization has been a well and widely used legislative instrument in the Congress for over 30 years.

In the considerations pending in Congress, sunset proposals will be refined with respect to (1) minimum review standards, (2) time schedules, (3) structures for grouping programs, (4) contents of reports, (5) definition of the individual entries in the program inventory and responsibility for such definitions, and (6) the nature of the "enforcement" mechanism to assure compliance to sunset procedures.

It should be expected that the sunset process will involve some learning and will grow only as its utility is established. The opportunities this provision creates for the evaluation community to provide a valuable service to the Congress, and the potential public benefits that could be derived from the improvement of public programs, could be substantial.

NOTES

1. Senators Joseph Biden and Patrick Leahy and Representative Butler Derrick are sponsors of measures dealing with improving congressional program review procedures. Many of their ideas have become incorporated in S.2 as it has evolved in the last three years. As of this writing, S.2 (Muskie) and S.1304 (Baucus-Tsongas) are before the Senate and HR2 (counterpart of S.2) and HR65 (Derrick) are before the House of Representatives; hearings have been completed in the Senate Committee on Governmental Affairs and the House Committee on Rules.

2. Other provisions not discussed here are: (1) for a three-year commission to study Federal government organization and operations; (2) requirements that the President submit with each annual budget request a grading of all Federal programs as either outstanding, satisfactory, or unsatisfactory and a ranking of the programs in each agency as to their degree of effectiveness; (3) additional review procedures for regulatory programs; and (4) floor procedures intended to avoid unintentional termination of programs as a result of unforeseen procedural problems.

3. The Federal subfunctions are approximately 90 categories into which the 1,000 appropriations accounts are classified for presentation in the budget submissions.

4. There are some exceptions to the sunset requirement, principally interest on the public debt, pension payments, and payment of tax refunds.

5. One distinction between "standing" and "special and select" committees used to be that only standing committees could report legislation authorizing programs. Some special and select committees now have such authority.

6. The other two are the Committee on Appropriations, which has authority to report appropriations bills, and the Committee on the Budget, which has authority to report concurrent resolutions on aggregate Federal spending, revenue, and deficit levels.

7. Another reason why authorizing bills are so called is that they usually contain provisions authorizing the enactment of appropriations. This is in addition to the more basic purpose of authorizing the program itself, i.e., the creation of the legal authority of the President or a secretary of a cabinet department to perform certain actions.

8. Committee jurisdictions in the Senate are set forth in Rule XXV of the Standing Rules of the Senate, available from the Committee on Rules and Administration.

9. The provisions governing the sizes of Senate committees, memberships, chairmanships, and service as ranking minority member are also in Rule XXV of the Standing Rules of the Senate, paragraphs 2 and 5.

10. Some committees have additional statutory positions.

Hillel Weinberg

Yale University

2

USING POLICY ANALYSIS IN
CONGRESSIONAL BUDGETING

It is universally acknowledged that it is hard to get Congress to use policy analysis (that is, empirical, explicit prospective or retrospective information on the effects of programs). In addition to numerous "practical" problems, Congress has lacked the appropriate organizational and procedural structures to consciously, systematically, or consistently use policy analysis. Dramatic changes were made possible by the Congressional Budget Act of 1974, which provided some of the necessary structure, but analysis is still not used to its full potential.[1] What were the opportunities presented in 1974? To what extent have they been pursued, and what will be their likely impact on the use of analysis by Congress?

The 1974 Budget Act created a congressional budget process, two budget committees, and a Congressional Budget Office.

The congressional budget process requires the setting, in budget resolutions, of spending targets for groups of programs. By setting these targets, Congress establishes priorities among the 17 budget "functions." Policy analysis can help the budget committee, when they consider their recommendations, to explicitly compare the desirability of different programs

---

AUTHOR'S NOTE: *This is a revised version of a paper presented at the annual meeting of the American Political Science Association, Washington, D.C., September 1-4, 1977. The original title announced in the 1977 APSA Annual Meeting Program was "Congressional Use of Policy Evaluation: Psychological and Organizational Perspectives." I am grateful for support provided during the interviewing period by the Institution for Social and Policy Studies, Yale University. The Brookings Institution generously granted me the use of their facilities during my stay in Washington. This research would have been impossible without the cooperation of numerous members of the professional staffs of the Congress of the United States. I gratefully acknowledge their candor and their helpfulness.*

and set the function targets more rationally than would otherwise be the case.

But the budget resolutions go beyond the establishment of target budget priorities. They also specify appropriate levels for overall federal outlays and receipts. (The expert fiscal "analysis" of the macroeconomic effects of setting those figures at particular levels is not what is meant by analysis in this essay. Here the word denotes knowledge of the more direct impacts of government programs on their beneficiaries, the operations of other programs, and so on.) Unlike the portions of the resolutions setting budget function targets, the figures on spending and receipts are binding. It is not in order for either house to consider any measure that would cause spending to exceed, or receipts to fall short of, the amounts specified in the resolution.

The budget committees are, of course, the structures within which priority setting and the use of analysis can proceed. The budget office's functions include the provision of analysis.

Much of the discussion that follows is based on a series of interviews conducted during the summer of 1976 with seven senior staff members of the budget committees. These interviews were conducted in the course of a larger project on Congress's use of evaluations of program impact. When relevant, the responses of members of the staffs of authorizing and appropriations committees will also be noted. The larger research project was limited to the use of analysis of human resources policy, but other policy areas were also taken up in some of the interviews.

PRIORITY SETTING IN THE BUDGET PROCESS IN THE FACE OF AMBIGUITY

Although early versions of the Budget Act, as it was being developed in both houses, contained detailed provisions for strong priority-setting mechanisms, they had been considerably weakened by the time the bills reached the floor. At that point, interest in using the budget process to set priorities seemed to be weaker than interest in using it to gain control over the overall size of the federal budget, matching income to expenditures, and other aspects of fiscal policy.

There is very little in either the act or the reports filed on it during its consideration that details just how the two budget committees are to go about drafting the budget resolutions. The most explicit provisions refer only to information that the committees are to receive: the "views and estimates" of the various legislative committees, the views of Members of

Congress and others as expressed in public hearings, and the annual report of the Congressional Budget Office. That annual report is to discuss, among other things, alternative allocations of the budget, and their "possible effects . . . on national growth and development."[3] At any rate, for the enlightenment of the plenum, the reports on the budget resolutions are to provide "information concerning the basis on which the amounts in the budget resolution were determined. . . . Each functional allocation is to be distributed between proposed and existing programs."[4]

Several factors account for the ambiguity of these provisions. One of them was the dispute, already mentioned, over the proper function of the budget process on the use of analysis by authorizing and appropriations appropriately concentrate on the "big picture," such as the proper size of the budget and other aspects of fiscal policy. Others propounded a much more activist role of them, advocating that they should include program-level targets for the appropriations process in the budget resolution. The House Rules Committee's report on the Budget Act recommended:

> a balanced course of action which gives Congress the benefit of knowing how spending totals have been derived . . . Congress would be able to leave to the appropriations process the determination of spending policy.[5]

The "balanced approach" that was adopted set the stage for uncertainty and conflict among actors in the budget process over the proper place of analysis. If little or no building of the budget details "from the ground up," with attention to the merit of particular programs, then there was no point in engaging in serious analysis. But if priority setting was a goal, then analysis might well be used.

A second factor was that priority setting in the new budget process would mean that some power would shift to the budget committee from other committees and that the power which the budget committees would gain would be directly related to the level of detail in which they would formulate their budget resolutions. The act's vagueness obfuscated this issue when it was being considered, in order not to provoke the various committees into opposition. Undoubtedly, it was wise to avoid being too blatant about a shift of power that might be acknowledged, in private, to be in the public interest.

The two explanations of the act's ambiguity on the question of the depth in which analysis could appropriately be pursued correspond to two general kinds of explanations of the impact of analysis: explanations that concern goals (in this case, of the budget committees and process) and what might be called "environmental" explanations.[6] Whether priority setting either is or is not considered an appropriate activity for the budget committee is a good example of an environmental (i.e., "practical," political, or organizational) concern.

The following discussion of the responses of committee staff members to questions about how and why analysis was or was not used in the budget process will begin with an exposition of the viewpoints of those staff members who opposed extensive priority setting by the budget committees. I will then proceed to the consideration of the environmental correlates of research utilization in the accounts of those who were oriented toward using it to help set priorities. Finally, I will consider the impact of the budget process on the use of analysis by authorizing and appropriations committees, and the future of analysis in the budget process.

OPPOSITION TO ANALYSIS IN THE BUDGET PROCESS

The two staff members who opposed a concentration on the priority-setting function by the committee (and on the use of analysis) made two arguments.

First, they said, the appropriate primary task of the committee was the establishment of "macro" budget figures—the size of the budget, the amount of revenues expected, the size of the deficit and the national debt—and a concentration on fiscal policy issues:

> No one else takes a look at what the outlay and revenue picture is going to be. . . . The focus here is on the big picture: that's how we get to aggregate numbers, not from the ground up.[7]

> Our basic macroeconomic consideration is "Are there enough jobs being produced with this high unemployment?" If we decide that there aren't, we formulate a resolution that will provide sufficient outlay to produce jobs.

Second, they said that decisions about budget levels for specific programs or even for fairly broad program areas ought to be made by the legislative and appropriations committees. They thought that was right either because it is wrong to have one committee making so many decisions, or (and this is an environmental explanation) because of a need to avoid "offending jurisdictions of other committees": "If this committee tries to 'line item' too much they'll say, 'Well, this is the end of the line—it's been nice, but we don't want you running everything.'"

Both of the staffers who disapproved of extensive involvement in priority setting mentioned specific spending issues that they said were not discussed in any detail, much less subjected to analysis, by their committees. In the House this list included the B-1. (It is, however, certain that defense programs with much lower costs were taken up by the Senate committee.) Evaluation of program impact per se was not opposed by these staffers; it was viewed as the job of legislative committees and as a process that would become more important as a result of the operation of the budget process:

> We put the overall limits, the targets . . . on the whole . . . government. . . . Things have to more or less fit into it; you hope you bring about a system that will more or less result in better evaluations of programs.

How would this work? The budget process results in the allocation of budgetary authority to subcommittees or programs by appropriations or legislative committees. The competition among subcommittees and other program advocates at the committee level was viewed as the primary and most appropriate place for the consideration of policy analysis. One staff member said that this competition for funds provides the only useful framework for the consideration of program analysis, the "only reason, other than rhetoric" to use it.

Both of the staff members predicted that the committee would get more deeply involved in "line items" as time went by. One reason cited was that it was necessary to be able to do so in order to justify passing the budget resolution to a sufficiently large coalition:

> This is a political committee. . . . Line items are how you're going to have to bargain with the members. You could avoid this for the first two years on the grounds that you were setting up the process, but now you've got to bargain on the issues. I would assume the members hope that they don't have to get into too many line items, because you'll just bargain yourself out of existence. . . . We may say, "We want this program because it's popular, we don't give a damn if the impact is very much or not."

They believed this path was dangerous because it would distract the committee from its original, macro-economic and budget-overseeing goals and because the committee would be seen as too powerful and would be abolished.

These respondents, explaining what they see as the committee's natural reluctance to involve itself in the use of analysis, first referred to the committee's appropriate goals, which do not necessarily require the use of analysis. To these they added political and environmental explanations, such as concern for the survival of the committee, as have been mentioned above.

WHY MOST STAFFERS FAVORED THE USE OF ANALYSIS

The rest of the staff members who were interviewed approved of a more active role for the committee in the priority-setting process and approved of the use of analysis to aid in that activity.

One staffer put the case for active priority setting using analysis succinctly:

> If all we're going to do is add on to the budget year in and year out, with never an evaluation of the existing programs, heaven help us, because we're growing geometrically. . . . I think there is a public groundswell [against it] . . . that's why Carter is the Democratic nominee. But you're not going to get a good senator to take a position unless he's very comfortable that the facts are with him. And the facts are going to have to be studies [of impact]. . . . We're pushing that way, and I hope we don't get killed in the process.

Another respondent asserted that the committee served the function of a center for disciplined thought and detailed analysis of important issues:

> An awful lot of junk comes out of Congress. There is a lot of stopping that ought to be done. The budget committee can do it, being the conscience of the Congress. Being outside the usual system of programs gives them a different perspective. . . . They can get a cost-benefit ratio and say, "We don't want to pay."

Despite staff interest in the explicit determination of spending priorities, relatively little attention was paid to this activity during the consideration of the 1977 budget resolutions. Alice Rivlin, Director of the Congressional Budget Office, observed, "I would have expected some discussion of these kinds of issues . . . but so far there hasn't been very much."[8] Most of the staffers explain inattention to priority setting and analysis as the result of the impact of environmental factors rather than to any question about the legitimacy or desirability of such activity.

ENVIRONMENTAL BARRIERS TO THE USE OF ANALYSIS

One impediment to the use of analysis cited by these staffers was the same as one mentioned earlier: the necessity to avoid dangerous encroachment on the territory of other committees. This need, however, was almost always expressed in practical terms, rather than in normative terms, or a mixture of the two, as was the case with the other respondents.

One staffer thought that the preeminent problem for the budget committee was the "turf" problem—what they would be allowed to do. Others did not attach such overriding importance to the problem, although one noted that the committee had to "walk pretty gingerly." He said that using policy analysis is "sort of unavoidable if we are to do our jobs well, but then problems with the authorizing and appropriating committees [become] unavoidable, too."

An example of the dangers of infringing on the jurisdiction of another committee (and of the political consequences involved in trying to use the results of analysis) was given by one Senate staffer who described a debate over a proposed tax credit for higher education expenses:

> We were the major opposition. We had a devastating memo against it. The provision was the product of only brief consideration in the Finance Committee and it was opposed by us on substantive grounds. Muskie spoke against it for half an hour or 45 minutes and many senators were in attendance. Long said that he was trying to help middle income people. At one point he was amenable to bringing the thing back to committee for another look, but the vote on the credit turned into a test on the whole bill, which we lost. We would never have let the vote on that turn into a test vote if we understood that the House would not accept it and that it would be taken out in the conference.

In fact, there were a number of losing attacks on provisions of the 1976 tax bill by the Senate Budget Committee, but the conference committee's version of it wound up conforming almost exactly to the relevant provisions of the budget resolution.[9]

There was a fairly prevalent feeling that because of restraints on encroachment, as well as time constraints, the committee could only involve itself in detailed analysis of a few programs or issues at any one time. It had to choose very carefully its areas "for special focus, for attack, if you will."

A Congressional Budget Office staffer observed that in some issue areas, legislative jurisdiction is pretty much concentrated in one subcommittee in each house. By the time that issue would reach the Budget Committee, it would be too late for their input to be very significant, most of the important issues having been decided except the appropriate budget level for the large set of programs of which the program in question is just one. In other areas (he used health as an example), there are a couple of committees with significant jurisdiction. Not only are potential policies more likely to be fluid and subject to change but also there are multiple access points and a competitive atmosphere that makes it more likely that analyses will be used to bolster a particular viewpoint. It was pointed out, though, that if the analyst is caught in the middle of a jurisdictional dispute, "no matter who wins, he gets it."

Another barrier to the impact of analysis is the tendency to make decisions incrementally, and the limited time available to conduct and consider analyses. The accounts of the staff, the substance of the budget reports and resolutions, and their very manner of preparation and presentation indicate clearly that what analysis is used at present is used to evaluate and compare only a sharply limited set of alternative decisions. A staffer illustrated pressures against the use of analysis:

> The Budget Committee tends to look in terms of "Medicare," "Medicaid," and "all other programs"—those which are not entitlements—as blocks, and they really haven't penetrated beneath that level at this point.

> There might be a very good study on, say, health manpower programs. The likelihood that our committee would spend more than a couple of minutes on health manpower is so slim—it's not worth the staff's time . . . to pay attention to that.

> At this point, we continue to rely on the judgment of the appropriations committee, which sets funding levels for [nonentitlement health] programs year in and year out. Perhaps at some point the committee will start making independent judgments, which hopefully will start out as marginal deviations from what appropriations is recommending. Just right now, _____ is on both budget and appropriations and he's very influential on us. So in the health grant programs, there is a link there in the form of an individual . . . who is going to play a major role in how that number comes out.

The shortage of appropriate analytical work, and the short time available to have the committee consider what does exist, is another kind of frustration experienced by the analytically oriented staff members. One of them described his problems obtaining appropriate information on two income maintenance programs and having the committee pay attention to it:

One problem is that the decisions that get made get made at the time that they do. There frequently aren't studies lying around you that you can grab and use. Take food stamps. Obviously, studies have been done . . . but at the time that the legislation was being considered, there were no good cost estimates of any of the alternative bills, much less analyses of their impact. So that left the members with, as the only alternative, the question of setting a politically acceptable number—"How much money do you want to cut out of the food stamp program?"

The black lung program has been ignored. . . . Well, it's a billion dollar program and it's worth worrying about. If there have been any good studies of what we ought to do with it, I've never seen them. . . . Now, they did not allow any money for new black lung legislation. I should have been able to give them a piece of paper ahead of time which said, "Here is the legislation. . . . Here are some other options. . .," but that wasn't done. There just isn't time. The black lung thing was one of maybe ten or twelve issues that we raised within the income security function. Of course, there are fifteen other functions that they have to set figures for, plus the revenues.

The majority staffs tended to be particularly distrustful of analytical work done by the executive branch. Both sides tended to mistrust work done by the authorizing committees on the grounds that they were too strongly committed promoting and justifying their programs.

Staff members frequently attributed the lack of influence of analysis to the fact that the aims of programs were vague, shifting, or not subject to measurement. One individual with responsibility for the analysis of educational programs spoke of his frustrations in these terms:

I have a perspective on . . . income maintenance programs . . . to test [a proposal] against and say, it's right or wrong. It's hard to do that same sort of thing in education because I just don't understand what we're doing or why we're doing what we're doing.

One staffer identified goals that were subject to multiple interpretations as the most serious barrier to the use of policy analysis. Three main classes of goals, which he saw as practically interchangeable at the whim of the advocates of human resources programs were (1) fiscal aid to institutions and jurisdictions, (2) anti-poverty and income redistribution, and (3) goals specific to the function of categorical programs.

A major debate during the summer of 1976 was focused on the "substitution effect" in public service employment programs, that is, whether or not those persons hired with money designed to reduce unemployment weren't just the original holders of their own jobs, who were now being paid with federal money (with the hiring entity pocketing the difference). He described the terms of the debate in the Senate Budget Committee:

> Senators who see [the public service jobs program] as a fiscal program are incredulous when you talk to them about substitution effects. They say, "If this program is not *designed* to produce a substitution effect, to provide financial relief to the cities, then what *is* it for?"
>
> Muskie comes back and argues that we're not out to help the cyclically unemployed, and that the jobs should be add-ons.
>
> The upshot is that the inconsistency remains. Because both sets of votes are needed to pass the program, it never gets resolved.
>
> What happens is that, eventually, other titles get added on and they say, "Now *this* is *really* categorical, maybe the other things are fiscal." In the last CETA Title I reauthorization, an income redistribution stance was taken almost explicitly. The Budget Committee sees Title I as a fiscal program by now—they say, "that's fine."
>
> The fiscal players are heavyweights—they don't like to be shut off.

Program evaluations are themselves said to result in shifting goals. One staffer said that attempts were made in the past to justify aid to federally impacted school districts on the grounds that the children whose schools received aid read better. "Eventually, they stopped trying to prove that—it was absurd. The lobbyists saw that they could get it through purely as a fiscal, political measure."

The education lobby is perceived as a particularly powerful group. That group among many others pressures the budget committee just as other committees are pressured.

WHEN ANALYSIS *IS* USED

Most of the staffers were able to provide examples of how they or the committee did use analysis. In such instances it was stated or implied that studies were available, that the timing was appropriate, and that there were no overwhelming pressures to approve a specific budget figure.

A careful interpretation of the descriptions of those circumstances can take us beyond a simple statement that there existed no major impediments to the use of analysis. It is clear that because of constant time pressures and the ready availability of fall back positions in the form of the previous year's budget figures, more than the mere absence of barriers was necessary to assure utilization. In many cases there had to be some special reason for analysis to be used.

Among the factors associated with increased receptivity to analysis is sharply increasing program costs. One staffer said that the rise in the cost of the food stamp program was "hitting people like a lightning bolt." He said that that had caused a lot of attention to be paid to an analysis demonstrating how hitherto unexamined relationships between elements of the benefit and eligibility structure of the food stamp program were responsible for the cost increases.

THE BUDGET COMMITTEES' INFLUENCE ON LEGISLATION FROM OTHER COMMITTEES

Upcoming program reauthorizations give the budget committees a chance to review, in a coherent fashion, the budgetary issues pertaining to various programs. Depending on the results of the review, the committee might intervene in the reauthorization or just hold on to its findings for use in the normal course of the budget process. Because the schedule for reauthorizations is known far in advance, the committees are able to arrange for studies to be performed for it on a timely basis. During the summer of 1976, the Senate Budget Committee was in the process of arranging for the production of a number of such studies, particularly from the Congressional Budget Office, on upcoming reauthorizations, such as the Elementary and Secondary Education Act.

The budget committees have a stake in all manner of legislation, not just in program reauthorizations. The passage of particular "reform" legislation may be assumed in the formulation of the budget resolutions. The committee may have to help get it passed. Similarly, unanticipated legislation that will inflate expenditures or otherwise upset established priorities may have to be opposed. In deciding which legislation to support or oppose, the committees and their chairmen rely on analysis. They may also use it in formulating their floor arguments if they wish to go beyond arguing for the preservation of the budget per se. One staffer said that his chairman said that he should be kept informed on all committee and floor action within the staffers' policy area:

"You keep track of what's happening, and if there are problems let me know; when I can influence, when I can testify, when I can write letters." It's a continuous, daily thing with him. Last night he was joking—he says he feels like a wind-up toy. We give him the stuff, and he goes out on the floor. It's not true that he's programmed—he wants to do it. He goes out on the floor day after day, and says, "this is under," "this is over," "this is in the resolution," "this is not in the resolution," "these are the implications of what you are going to do." Just a routine thing. They call him "the Professor."

When these interviews were conducted, a committee-backed proposal to cut the 1% "kicker" (an extra increase added to inflation adjustments in certain federal pensions) had just lost in the House under suspension-of-the-rules procedures (requiring a two-thirds vote). Although the vote was lost, a number of those who were interviewed referred to the kicker as a good example of committee influence based on analyses of long-term costs. The committee had assumed its elimination in the budget resolution and had backed the measure in the Post Office Committee. One staffer said, "We did a great job . . . but there is on the loose an association of retired federal employees."

Large program increases or decreases proposed in the President's budget give the committees an opportunity to use analysis in exercising their independent judgment about appropriate funding levels. Presidential initiatives of this kind may be accepted by the committees in whole or in part. It is less difficult for them to achieve a decrease in funding by partially approving a deep presidential cut than by trying to sell their own justification for such a cut. The House Budget Committee appeared to use this approach when it recommended funding levels for nonentitlement health programs.

The staff believes that a long run tightening of the budget situation will lead to the increased use of analysis. In the face of demands for the enactment of expensive legislation initiatives and the likelihood of only small increases in the size of the budget, there was some talk of an era of substitution of more effective for less effective programs based on the results of analysis. "We'll see deeper analysis of what's good and what's bad about existing programs. . . . You're not going to have Congress have no new initiatives for five years."

THE IMPACT OF THE BUDGET PROCESS
ON ANALYSIS IN OTHER COMMITTEES

The budget process affects the use of analysis in committees other than the budget committees. The changes result from the pressure of budget limitations sharpened by the budget process and from the series of formal actions required by the budget process.

Authorizing committees in each house must make reports, each March, to their budget committees. These reports contain suggested budget levels for programs under their jurisdiction as well as the committees' legislative plans insofar as they have budgetary implications. The budget committee staffs and some staff members of the authorizing committees expect that this annual exercise, which requires committees to make their legislative and spending priorities explicit, will result in an increase in the use of analysis in the authorizing committees. One committee was praised by a budget staffer for having made good progress, in its 1976 report, toward providing "real numbers, not just balloon numbers." This praise was impressive, since it came immediately after he had criticized the staff of that same committee as being difficult to work with because of their ideological commitment to the programs under their jurisdiction. Another staffer said that he thought that the recommendations of the same committee were unrealistically high, but attributed that to the short time the committee had to prepare its report. Such an attribution implies a presumption of intellectual and analytic honesty on the part of the authorizing committee.

The procedures another authorizing committee used to prepare its recommendations appear to be less in conformity with the ideal of utilizing analysis. A member of the staff of that committee was asked whether the committee set priorities among its programs with the help of research on their impact. He replied, in effect, that their decision process was largely incremental and nonanalytical.

> This committee . . . doesn't operate like the Budget Committee. . . . What it does is consider the needs of each program and build its recommendations that way. Actually, there is some compromise along the way, because in order to get a majority vote . . . there has to be some give and take, but basically, we derive totals in that fashion. What enters into the judgment is not a budget consideration. What generally goes into it is "How much did we spend last year? . . . What do you really think we got for it last year? . . . What can the administration effectively use next year?" Most of that involves calculating what the program objectives are, rather than weighing the evidence.

One committee responded to the budget process by setting up a new staff unit attached to the committee central staff. This unit combines budget and program evaluation functions, which its staff views as inextricable:

> This [evaluation] material underpins the recommendations that we are required to make.

> The Budget Act has changed the game in this country. . . . We're doing this because it's going to be important as the budget process becomes more refined, as we have to justify our programs against judgments and studies from other sources. So I view it as not just a good thing for us, but as a survival mechanism.

The staffer quoted above characterized the utilization of evaluation by his committee up to the time of the interview as minimal. He anticipated that the unit he worked in would help to trigger an expansion of the use of evaluation beyond that needed for the fulfillment of the requirements of the budget process.

Units such as his are set up for the explicit purpose of (to use the words of another authorizing committee staffer) "playing the budget game": to counter the "computer mystique" of the "technocrats" at the Congressional Budget Office or the budget committees who may be working from unsympathetic assumptions. Nevertheless, their establishment will strengthen the hands of the analytically oriented within the committees, since they will tend to staff those units and control the committees' own computer systems. Since the preparation of the reports to the budget committees are a responsibility of the committee as a whole, some recentralization of power into the hands of committee chairmen may occur in decentralized committess.

The appropriations committees' staffs held varying views on the impact of the budget process on their operations. One individual viewed it as of no real consequence, with its main effect being the reduction of the rolls of the unemployed by a few hundred. The others indicated that they thought that it would lead to some diminution of the importance of the appropriations committees, although surprisingly they did not unanimously deplore that possibility. Some felt that the budget committee would help keep spending from increasing too rapidly or unjustifiably when their own committees said that the spending levels set in the budget for human services were so high as to be "unattainable," and that the appropriations committees would come under (and succumb to) undue pressure to appropriate up to the limit of the budget resolution.

CONCLUSIONS

Anyone who thought that congressional behavior would be revolution-ized by the advent of the new budget process has reason to be disappointed. In its 1976 incarnation, the process was marked by inattention to priority-setting issues. Analyses of program impact could not be credited with having influenced many important decisions of the budget committees. Rather, incremental changes from current policy dominated budget de-cisions.

However, there are several signs of analytic life being transmitted from within the budget process. There *is* evidence that some analytic work was taken seriously by the budget committees. There is awareness on the part of the staff of the barriers to utilization and of some aids to utilization as well. An apparatus—the Congressional Budget Office and the budget committees—has been set up whose organizational essence (most of its members agree) is tied up with the use of analysis. Self-consciously and purposefully, staff members generate new analyses, seek out and assimilate work done elsewhere, and try to bring the common knowledge of their individual professions into focus in order to help congressional decision makers. Under the prodding of the budget process and its potential danger to the established order, there has been some expansion of legislative committee analytic and oversight activities.

While the many environmental barriers to the utilization of analysis seem formidable, there is reason to believe that their impact will diminish in the relatively short term with a combination of the effects of committee effort, the passage of time, and the *force majeur* of tight budget ceilings.

For a variety of reasons, then, the budget committees will become more and more deeply involved in using analysis and making line-item decisions. Their skill and timing in moving in that direction, and the extent to which its commitment to priority-setting remains strong, will be important to the maintenance of the macro-economic and macro-budget functions of the committees as well as to the success of their priority-setting function.

In the most optimistic scenario of the committee's future, each of them will gradually become involved in detailed budget analysis under the appropriate environmental conditions. Serious opposition to the idea of their setting (or even proposing) budget priorities will have quieted down, and the committee will be deferred to by and large. The committees' judgments are ultimately made for the sake of institutional maintenance, in order to save Congress and the nation from their lack of rationality. The committees will, presumably self-consciously, become, in David Mayhew's phrase, "control committees."[10] In the tradition of the appropriations committees and the House Ways and Means Committee, they would attempt to discipline the entire body for the sake of a broader national interest and institutional survival.

The second possibility involves the committees' losing their will to act as checks on the rest of the institution. Control committees can serve such a function for a long time, but they may eventually come to be permeated or come to identify with unjustifiable claims on national treasure. If the budget committees' members lost (or never really had) the will to act to determine budget priorities as direct checks on their colleagues, they would probably strategically withdraw to a position of setting overall budget figures and only give sketchy accounts of how they arrived at those figures. They would rely on the pressure of those ceilings, the administration's internal mechanisms, and on competition within the authorizing and appropriations committees to provide any necessary incentives to economy and efficiency.

A third possible course of events is that the committees will attempt to set line-item figures before clearing away the critical environmental barriers to the use of analysis and the setting of priorities. If the justifications offered for their actions are not convincing, or if their actions are politically clumsy, the result could be a defeat of a budget resolution or even a rebellion against the budget process and a return to the old system.

Given (1) the strong yet cautious non-"prioritizing" bent of the staff, (2) the prospects for a lessened impact of barriers to the utilization of analysis, (3) broad agreement that restraints on the size of the federal budget are necessary, and (4) the relative weakness of other control committees, the first scenario that was described has a reasonable chance of being fulfilled and remaining valid for a number of years. Congress has created for itself an opportunity to enhance its power and the national interest through the use of policy analysis to help set national priorities; it stands a good chance to be able to capitalize on that opportunity.

NOTES

1. Some very useful and cogent discussions of the utilization of analysis by Congress have recently appeared in the literature. All of them were written between the passage of the Budget Act and the conclusion of the first full-fledged congressional budget cycle in 1976, and most find some grounds for cautious optimism. They include a number of articles appearing in

a special section on "Clients and Analysts: Congress," in the Spring 1976 issue of *Policy Analysis* (2:2) (Roger H. Davidson, "Congressional Committees: The Toughest Customers," pp. 299-323; Robert H. Haveman, "Policy Analysis and the Congress: An Economist's View," pp. 235-250; Charles O. Jones, "Why Congress Can't Do Policy Analysis (or words to that effect)," pp. 251-264; Allen Schick, "The Supply and Demand for Analysis on Capitol Hill," pp. 215-234; and James A. Thurber, "Congressional Budget Reform and New Demands for Policy Analysis," pp. 197-214), as well as Joel D. Aberbach, "The Development of Oversight in the United States Congress: Concepts and Analysis," in *Techniques and Procedures for Analysis and Evaluation: A Compilation of Papers Prepared for the Commission on the Operation of the Senate* (Washington, D.C.: U.S. Government Printing Office, 1977), and Allen Schick, "Evaluating Evaluation: A Congressional Perspective," in *Legislative Oversight and Program Evaluation: A Seminar Sponsored by the Congressional Research Service* (Washington, D.C.: U.S. Government Printing Office, 1976).

3. U.S., Congress, Senate, Report 93-924, Conference Report on HR7130, P. 54.

4. Ibid., p. 59.

5. U.S., Congress, House, Report 93-658, to accompany HR7130, p. 34.

6. Cf. Thurber, op. cit., "My guess is that their propensity to use policy analysis will be limited by environmental constraints and the goals of the members," p. 210. Another explanation is that analyses maybe misperceived and consequently mistakenly interpreted by Members or their staffs. Such misinterpretations are inadvertent and subconscious, but there is evidence that serious misperceptions do occur. An investigation of such misperceptions and their impact on congressional policy making was undertaken as one part of the larger project of which this study is also a part. The results will be reported in the author's forthcoming dissertation "Policy analysis: its impact on congressional policy making."

7. All unattributed quotations are excerpts from transcripts of interviews with members of the professional staffs of Congress. All respondents are referred to in the masculine to help preserve their anonymity.

8. Joel Havemann, "The Congressional Budget—On Time and a Long Time Coming," National Journal, September 18, 1976, p. 1307.

9. Ibid.

10. David R. Mayhew, *Congress: The Electoral Connection* (New Haven, Yale University Press, 1974), pp. 147-150.

3

Keith E. Marvin
Program Analysis Division,
U.S. General Accounting Office

EVALUATION FOR
CONGRESSIONAL COMMITTEES
The Quest for Effective Procedures

There are technical reasons why program evaluation has often failed to live up to its promise. However, in this author's opinion, the reason most damaging to legislators' confidence has been the lack of a single generally accepted definition of program evaluation. As a consequence, legislators all too frequently have been victims of inflated expectations whose disappointment has been exacerbated by communication obstacles between them and evaluators.

Lack of definition and lack of communication have been common because evaluation has been viewed as a collection of techniques which could be called upon to solve a generally stated problem. No magic assemblage of techniques, however, can enhance legislator confidence. The only basis for improvement is use of a process whereby those who are expected to use evaluation results can be included in the crucial phases of the enterprise. Further, the successful evaluation process can be tailored to support policy need if it observes a generally recognized and accepted conceptual model of evaluation. The model must embrace the organizing principles of shared definition and regularities of communication necessary to implement the principles effectively.

CURRENT PERCEPTIONS OF EVALUATION:
WHERE DID THEY ORIGINATE?

Program evaluation became government-wide in the late 1960s in response to demand, particularly from the Congress, to learn whether major new social programs were achieving their intended objectives. Many of these programs were implemented through grants to state and local governments. Those nonfederal entities also became involved in evaluation of the impact of federal programs—on both individuals and communities.

Moreover, federal program managers required evaluation information to tell them whether grantees were implementing programs as intended. This requirement led to extensive monitoring of local projects. It also led to construction of complex management information systems in order to manage federal reporting requirements related to evaluation. These systems provided mounds of detailed operational statistics but little information about impacts of programs on individuals and communities.

The demand for impact assessments of federal programs led to many attempts to gather data outside of established program management channels and information systems. Packaged as studies, these attempts relied heavily on the methods of social science and social research. Many emphasized use of experimental methods which measured the results of ongoing programs as though everything in their environments was held constant. In a laboratory test, such methods are used successfully to assess the difference between those individuals affected by a treatment and those in an untreated group. However, the experimental method has been less effective in producing evaluation information for policy-making and may be of limited use in assessing broad-scope programs and activities.

AN APPROACH TO DEFINITION OF EVALUATION

Program evaluation can be viewed as the use of various systematic approaches to find out how well a program has worked and what options are available for improving its performance. However, defining evaluation as one or more techniques focuses attention on techniques rather than on utilization of the evaluation results.

A useful utilization focus is predicated upon the concept that program evaluation is a function intended to assist future policy and management decisions; that it assists such decisions by appraising the manner and extent to which programs are achieving their stated objectives; that it accounts for the program performance perceptions and expectations of responsible public officials, interest groups, and/or the public; and that it tracks other significant effects of either a desirable or undesirable character.

Utilization-focused program evaluation does not restrict the value of such research to management alone. Evaluation, however, fails when it does not assist future policy and management decisions. For best results, knowledge should be exchanged among activities called program evaluation and activities using other approaches to analysis.

The foregoing view of program evaluation has emerged from GAO's review of current literature and its own program evaluation experience related to program oversight and accountability. This view is consistent with evolution of recent thinking about the use of evaluative analysis. For example, Schultze (1968) stated that "program evaluation is a means of gaining knowledge retrospectively about production functions in order to improve initial predictions, to modify and adjust program design, and to screen out relatively ineffective alternatives." Schultze also identified a dilemma which requires attention: "this latter aspect [ineffective alternatives] causes difficulties, since those in charge of the particular program have an obvious interest in producing favorable evaluations. There is no automatic way to prevent a bias in structuring evaluation studies and in interpreting their results." More recently this dilemma has been well stated from the program managers' point of view by Chelimsky (1977):

> Many of the agency managers, who are to be held accountable, are greatly concerned about the methods and processes of their accountability, and about the ability of the evaluation to provide the conclusive determination of program effectiveness upon which the establishment depends. Program managers are disturbed not so much at the idea of accountability, as at their perception of the likely quality of that accountability, the political aspects of that accountability, and the possibility that premature, preliminary, unfair or inconclusive evaluation findings, distorted or even inaccurately reported by the press, could result in the unwarranted demise of a promising program.

In sum, Chelimski stated, "the congressional use of agency evaluation for any of the Congress' purposes will depend upon the acceptance of evaluation by agency managers."

IMPROVING THE QUALITY OF EVALUATIONS: CONGRESSIONAL INITIATIVES

The Congress recognized its need for more defensible program evaluations in the Congressional Budget Act of 1974. Among other things, it required that the Comptroller General recommend methods of review and evaluation of all federal programs. GAO has responded to this requirement by developing and issuing a series of guidelines for making program evaluation more useful for decision-makers. These guidelines are of several types: (1) those of government-wide applicability; for example, suggestions for congressional oversight outlining an approach to arriving at a reasonable agreement between the Congress and the executive agencies on expectations, objectives, and achievements for programs; (2) those containing frameworks for analysis in broad program or functional areas; for example, suggested methods to deal with uncertainty in estimates of costs and benefits from water resource projects; and (3) frameworks for analysis contained in reports or reviews of specific programs; for example, suggested methods of comparing the cost and performance of federally subsidized rental housing programs and other federal housing programs.

GAO has a practice of issuing its guidelines as exposure drafts in order to obtain widely representative comments from persons in federal, state, and local government as well as academic and research institutions. Revision based on these comments increases acceptance of GAO guidelines when issued in final form. Many leaders in the evaluation community have welcomed the existence of this GAO focal point as a means to synthesize and organize generally accepted positions of the evaluation community. Figure 1 lists the guidelines issued to date in the first two categories discussed above and presents examples of the GAO's third developmental category.

A MODEL OF THE EVALUATION FUNCTION FOR PROGRAM MANAGEMENT

It will take time to improve evaluation methods and participatory processes throughout government so that evaluation products will be viewed by program management as an equitable measurement of program performance. Both the Office of Management and Budget and the General Accounting Office are committed to the idea that program evaluation must be of use to program management. OMB has stated (Granquist, 1977) that "first program evaluation is basically a tool for improved program management. Thus, agency heads and their program managers must have the prime responsibility for evaluation decisions." Thus, GAO is basing current development of evaluation guidelines on two premises:

GUIDELINES OF GENERAL SCOPE

Date Issued:	Title
September 1976	Evaluation And Analysis To Support Decisionmaking, PAD-76-9
September 1976	Evaluating Federal Programs: An Overview For The Congressional User, PAD-76-30
October 1978	Status And Issues: Federal Program Evaluation, PAD-78-83
November 1977	Finding Out How Programs Are Working: Suggestions For Congressional Oversight, PAD-78-3
January 1979	Guidelines For Model Evaluation, PAD-79-17

FRAMEWORKS OR GUIDELINES FOR BROAD PROGRAM OR FUNCTIONAL AREAS

Issued:	
June 1977	Government Regulatory Activity: Justifications, Processes, Impacts, And Alternatives, PAD-77-34
May 1978	Federal Credit Assistance, PAD-78-31
June 1978	Better Analysis Of Uncertainty Needed For Water Resource Projects, PAD-78-67
August 1978	U.S. Foreign Relations And Multinational Corporations: What's The Connection?, PAD-78-58
October 1978	Audits And Social Experiments: A Report Prepared For The U.S. General Accounting Office By The Committee On Evaluation Research, Social Science Research Council, PAD-79-1
October 1979	Assessing Social Program Impact Evaluations: A Checklist Approach, PAD-79-2

EXAMPLES OF PROGRAM REVIEW REPORTS CONTAINING FRAMEWORKS FOR PROGRAM EVALUATION AND ANALYSIS

Issued:	
January 1978	Section 236 Rental Housing—An Evaluation With Lessons For The Future, PAD-78-13. (A related framework limited to costs was contained in a prior report "Comparative Analysis Of Subsidized Housing Costs", PAD-76-44, July 1976)
February 1979	Better Understanding Of Wetland Benefits Will Help Water Bank And Other Federal Programs Achieve Wetland Preservation Objectives, PAD-79-10

Figure 1

(1) program evaluation is a fundamental part of effective program administration, and (2) the best test of the effectiveness of the evaluation function is improvement in program performance.

The OMB and GAO policies both stress that the success of program evaluation must be tied to the success of programs themselves. Reviewing the success of evaluation involves more than activities which include the word *evaluation* in their title. Participation in evaluation by program management must be examined as well.

Evaluation is a particular application of the scientific method. Scientific method and scientific management are no mystery to most program managers.

Program managers understand evaluation best if it is not oriented toward problem solving or testing whether new program ideas are working. Accordingly, we must design an evaluation function to support program managers, or those managers will not be supportive of evaluation. If the evaluation function gives them information they need, managers will probably cooperate in providing other desirable information to meet executive and legislative evaluation needs.

To guide an evaluation function capable of implementing utilization-focused, program-oriented evaluation, we have developed six tentative criteria. These criteria incorporate GAO's earlier work for the Congress on improving information for oversight. They include means to assess the combined performance of evaluation activities and program management. In our surveys of agency evaluation processes, these criteria are being tested to determine how well they serve the needs of program management.

For example, we need to know how to determine:

- Whether Congress and the executive accept management's statement of objectives and expectations for the program (i.e., is there an understanding in terms of measurable and realistic definitions of program objectives?).

- Whether program activities which make objectives and expectations achievable are in place (i.e., does the program as implemented make the objectives plausible—is there an evaluable program?).

In our development of evaluation methodology, we are testing and demonstrating how performance of various evaluable programs can be measured. This work involves use of known techniques such as simulation. It involves also the identification and development of promising approaches for dealing with such evaluation problems as multiple and possibly conflicting program goals.

It is essential that evaluability and program performance deficiencies be corrected over time (i.e., the evaluation function is more than a collection of unrelated ad hoc studies; rather, it should be a function containing a memory of related indicators from which the trends over time can be obtained). This will hopefully foster updating over time of the program objectives and expectations for program performance.

Program management must be directly involved in the planning of evaluations and in the interpretation of results. The relationship of the evaluation function to program decision-making by and accountability of program management is presented schematically in Figure 2.

An additional and important characteristic of the evaluation function may be termed program design analysis. This activity requires staff with diverse skills, for example, to retrieve data, to estimate costs of options, and to simulate options if appropriate. This part of the evaluation function could be performed by various groups. What is essential is the competence to undertake the necessary preliminary analysis and to present the results as options for the program manager to use in improving the program. This eclectic analysis uses techniques similar to those used in policy analysis for considering major national objectives although their scope may be narrowed in program evaluation efforts. It is important that the needs of decision-makers or groups of decision-makers in particular settings of government be considered in deciding on the scope of such analysis.

ADDITIONAL CONSIDERATIONS FOR POLICY RELEVANT EVALUATION

Evaluations most useful for purposes of policy-making are unlikely to result where the evaluation activity is serving solely the immediate needs of program managers. For example, GAO found in its assessment of evaluation of programs in the Department of Transportation (U.S. General Accounting Office, 1979b) that "in most cases the system is decentralized and evaluative activities, with the exception of a few legislatively-mandated studies, are aimed primarily at providing program managers with information on operational and technical deficiencies. . . . Most of the studies compared the status of a program's operations to what had been planned."

With good communication between policy-makers and program managers, however, it seems reasonable that the appropriate needs of

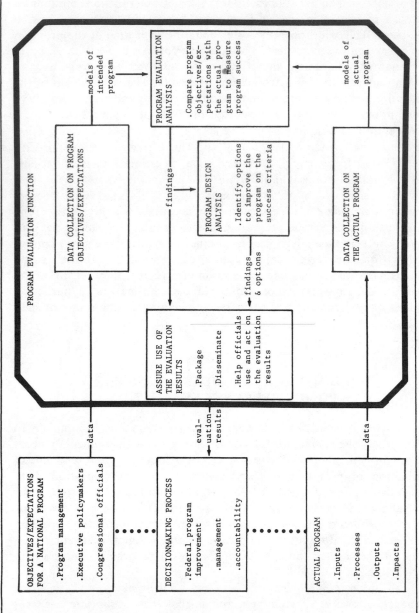

Figure 2: Model of the Program Evaluation Function

both groups can be met by evaluations when research designs incorporate the six criteria being field tested by GAO. There are many questions which would probably be of equal interest to the Congress and a program manager. For example, in the case of soil and water conservation, several questions are likely to be of interest to both parties:

—What are the purposes of each program?

—Are the delivery mechanisms or unique features of each program reflected in the list of purposes?

—Is each purpose essential to soil and water conservation, or does it relate to some broader purpose? If the latter, to what extent should soil and water conservation to be expected to contribute to the broader purpose?

—Which conservation problems cannot be adequately described with existing data or estimating procedures and what steps are being taken to fill these voids? How do the activities of soil and water conservation supporting programs correspond to filling these voids?

These questions were among a list developed in a study of information needed for oversight of eighteen soil and water conservation programs. It is clear that similar questions in other issue areas would be of interest to the Congress and the executive. Their determination is dependent in large part upon a bargaining process similar to that used in all multilateral decision-making.

The link between analytic and political process is optimistically described by Schultze:

We can agree with Lindblom that the purpose of the advocacy process and political bargaining is to reach decisions about specific programs in the context of conflicting and vaguely known values. Systematic analysis makes a major and essential contribution to this process by forging links between general values and specific program characteristics—links that are immediately and directly evident only in the simplest cases. It forges these links, first, by determining social production functions that relate program inputs to program outputs, and second, by translating general values into operationally specific objectives against which the outputs can be evaluated. Analysis of both objectives and production functions must be a simultaneous process in which better understanding of production functions clarifies objectives, and a clearer knowledge of objectives stimulates the development of alternative production functions.

A less optimistic view of evaluation design bargaining was stated recently by Wildavsky (1978): "viewed from the standpoint of bureau interest, programs, to some extent, are negotiable; some can be increased and others decreased while keeping the agency on an even keel or, if necessary, adjusting it to less happy times without calling into question its very existence."

Currently, various proposals for oversight reform have in common the requirement that similar programs be examined together. Such proposals favor the interests of more globally thinking policy-makers over detail-conscious program managers.

Two additional criteria should be considered by evaluators to reconcile the different points of view when multiple program groupings are under review.

—There should be agreement between policy-makers and program managers on the grouping of similar programs which are relevant to the policy question under evaluation.

—Measures must exist by which the programs in the grouping can be compared analytically.

Those additional considerations should help to determine whether the evaluation process conducted within an agency is likely to be able to provide the information expected for policy decisions. These criteria can assist policy evaluation which is independent of the mission of a particular program.

Some programs may be too small to provide all of the information needed to assess a national objective. The Water Bank Program in the Department of Agriculture, for example, is too restricted in scope for fully understanding wetland preservation dynamics and cost-benefit relationships. GAO (1979a) reported recently that the Water Bank Program administered by the Agricultural Stabilization and Conservation Service is not as effective as it could be in preserving wetlands. The report recommended that Congress change the Water Bank Act (Public Law-91-559) to increase the secretary's flexibility in administering the program by giving him (1) greater discretion as to what wetlands should be preserved and (2) the ability to adjust payment rates during the course of the ten-year agreements made under the program. Several areas were identified where USDA should improve its understanding of the way the program operates to increase its effectiveness and efficiency.

In this case, GAO's report took special care to point out that wetland preservation is an issue that goes beyond USDA's Water Bank Program. It was noted that the Department of Interior, the Army Corps of Engineers, the Environmental Protection Agency, and the Water Resources Council are also involved in wetland protection.

Illustrating the need for useful existing evaluation measures in the report on multiprogram assessments, GAO stated that an apparent emphasis in the efforts of these agencies favoring the value of wetlands to waterfowl and other wildlife may cause neglect of other wetland values such as flood control, pollution and sediment control, and groundwater supply. Information on these values is lacking and such measures as relate to them are not well coordinated between the several interested agencies. To remedy the situation it was recommended that a coordinated data collection and research effort be carried out under the leadership of the Water Resources Council.

Some programs may be too large and need to be disaggregated to provide policy relevant evaluations. For example, the scope of the activities funded under Title I of the Elementary and Secondary Education Act of 1965 may be too large for consideration of single mission objectives such as improving reading or mathematical ability. A congressionally mandated evaluation of the federal government's Compensatory Education Program conducted pursuant to Title I is discussed in Chapter 8 of this volume.

SUMMARY

Given extensive skepticism about the usefulness of evaluation and the frequent failure of evaluation to provide policy relevant information, the concerns of program managers have been identified as crucial to effective evaluation and their needs must be met. A procedure has been suggested whereby the needs of program managers and policy-makers can be reconciled for more successful evaluation efforts.

REFERENCES

CHELIMSKY, E. (1977) "Statement of the Head, Program Evaluation, and Director, Planning and Policy Analysis, MITRE Corporation." Oversight hearings on the scope and extent of the federal government's efforts to evaluate its programs (October 27).
GRANQUIST, W. (1977) "Statement of the Associate Director for Management and Regulatory Policy, Office of Management and Budget." Oversight hearings on the scope and extent of the federal government's efforts to evaluate its programs (October 6).
SCHULTZE, C. L. (1968) The Politics and Economics of Public Spending. Washington, DC: The Brookings Institution.

U.S. General Accounting Office (1979a) "Better Understanding of Wetland Benefits Will Help Water Bank and Other Federal Programs Achieve Wetland Preservation Objectives [PAD-79-10]." Washington, DC: Government Printing Office.

——— (1979b) "Evaluation of Programs in the Department of Transportation—An Assessment [PAD-79-13]." Washington, DC: Government Printing Office.

WILDAVSKY, A. (1978) "A budget for all seasons? Why the traditional budget lasts." Public Administration Rev. (November/December): 501-509.

Carlotta Joyner Young
Pennsylvania State University
Joseph Comtois
U.S. General Accounting Office

4

INCREASING CONGRESSIONAL
UTILIZATION OF EVALUATION

There is a nearly unanimous agreement that program evaluation activities should aid decisionmaking (Weiss, 1972: 10). Most definitions of program evaluation, in fact, include some reference to its intended use. For example, *Issue Area Evaluation Guideline and Methodology* (Program Plan, 1978) issued by the General Accounting Office defines program evaluation as "the process of appraising the manner and extent to which programs are

(1) achieving their stated objectives,
(2) meeting the performance perceptions and expectations of responsible Federal officials and other interested groups, and/or
(3) producing other significant effects of either a desirable or undesirable character,

in order to assist future policy and management decisions [italic mine]" (1978: 1-4). Yet writers have been almost as unanimous in pointing out that evaluation results often seem not to be used by decisionmakers (e.g., Cox, 1977; Wholey et al., 1970). The question is: Why not? And, as an obvious extension: What should be done to enable program evaluation activities to meet their use mandate?

AUTHORS' NOTE: *An earlier version of this article was prepared in the summer of 1978 while the first author was employed in the Program Analysis Division of the U.S. General Accounting Office, and was presented at the Evaluation Research Society annual meeting, November 1978, Washington, DC. That version benefited greatly from comments by Donald C. Pelz and Carol H. Weiss. Opinions expressed in the article are those of the author, however, and do not necessarily reflect those of the General Accounting Office or individual reviewers.*

This chapter presents criteria fundamental for federal evaluation policy. Described in some detail in order to promote congressional capacity to utilize evaluation efforts, such criteria have been formulated as a result of extensive investigation conducted in 1978 by the General Accounting Office. The investigation featured interviews with selected government officials. It also featured an extensive review of the literature concerned with utilization of evaluation. The utilization criteria drawn from the findings of the investigation are presented below. The findings are set forth in the Appendix to this chapter.

UTILIZATION CRITERIA: IMPLICATIONS FOR EVALUATION POLICY

The synthesis *formulated by GAO* suggests four specific implications and related criteria for evaluation policy:

(1) Evaluations must be utilization-focused. Planning for utilization must be an integral part of evaluation planning from the beginning.

(2) Criteria for assessing the use-relevance of program evaluations are relative rather than absolute. They are themselves a proper topic for negotiation and agreement between evaluators and decision-makers.

(3) An important factor in utilization is an interactive process between decision-makers and evaluators. Such a process can assure that decision-makers are committed to use and that evaluators will produce useful findings. Yet it must be accomplished without infringing on the necessary independent stance of the evaluator.

(4) Other factors such as question appropriateness, methodology, and dissemination are also important. But adequacy on those dimensions is made more likely by the interactive process.

Utilization Focus of Evaluation

Considering the use of evaluation findings is not an activity that belongs at the end of the study. Dissemination of results is an important issue, involving consideration of communication medium, style, recipients, role of the evaluator in "marketing" findings, and more. But dissemination does not equal or guarantee utilization. The larger issue is that the best dissemination procedure available cannot make up for an absence of planning *from the beginning* that these results be useful, and incorporating in the evaluation design all that is known about enhancing utilization.

Criteria for Assessing Use

Evaluation findings are, and should be, only one among several inputs to the decision-making process. The process, including even the choice of programs to be evaluated, the measure used, etc., is inextricably a political activity. Many different aspects and sources of information must be considered, all from the value perspective of the decision-makers. Consequently, the assumption that use can be defined only as actual program changes in the direction of evaluation recommendations is certainly naive.

How, then, can use be defined? And how can criteria for assessing the use-relevance of an evaluation activity or system be determined?

It has been proposed that utilization can vary along the several dimensions of

—what is used?
—what type of use occurs?
—by whom?
—by how many people?
—confidence in deriving an impact-evaluation association,
—strength and direction of impact, and
—immediacy/timing of use.

An early step in developing an evaluation plan should be clarifying what kinds of use will be the primary goal, i.e., what the criteria for assessing use will be. Some dimensions will be more relevant than others, but at a minimum some consideration should be given to the questions of (1) whether issues or programs will be the use focus ("what is used?") and (2) what groups of users/decision-makers will be served ("by whom?"). Since use criteria are relative rather than absolute, an evaluation study or plan should not be "faulted," when appraising its adequacy, for not meeting standards of use no one ever intended it to meet.

Evaluators-Decision-Makers Interaction

Commitment of one or more persons in the decision-making structure to use of the evaluation appears to be a crucial factor in its success, especially in instrumental use. And that commitment seems to hinge on active involvement of decision-makers with evaluators in the evaluation process. This seems to be true whether the users are at the congressional level, on the agency policy level, or actively involved in program management.

Several reasons for the relationship between involvement and use have been proposed. Decision-makers' commitment to use involves them personally with a sense of "ownership" of the data. This interaction also increases the probability that the right question will have been asked. Also, users are more likely to trust the data and to be less threatened by them.

There is more agreement on the need for such a process than on suggestions for how to accomplish it. And a variety of potential limitations to such a process could easily be listed. For one thing, there are many potential users of an evaluation beyond those directly involved in commissioning an evaluation. These secondary users cannot all be involved in planning, or even identified. Even the primary users who participate in deliberations at the outset of a study may have gone on to other positions by the time the study nears its end. And this process may require opening up new channels of communication which pose threats to the existing bureaucratic structure.

In addition, such a process will be most successful when the participants are involved because they *choose* to be (as has usually been the case in the studies cited). To move to a recommendation that an interactive process be formalized in some cases overlooks that aspect of the "personal factor." More research is needed on the personal characteristics that have led some decision-makers and evaluators to operate in this way in the past (i.e., the attitudes, skills, previous experiences, etc.) and the structural aspects that have encouraged or allowed it (social norms, incentive structure, etc.).

Nevertheless, it may be helpful to consider an interactive process involving evaluators and decision-makers. How could it be accomplished? When should it be undertaken? And who should be involved?

HOW TO DO IT?

Several different interactive approaches have been demonstrated or suggested in the literature.

There has been considerable advocacy of the data of the evaluator as a change agent (c.f., *Evaluation* magazine). This literature is typically addressing the interaction between evaluators and program managers, especially in the area of mental health. One example of this approach is that of Davis and Salasin (1975) proposing the A VICTORY technique to assess an organization's receptiveness to new information and then working with program practitioners and managers to facilitate that use.

Patton (1978) stressed that his comprehensive approach to "utilization-focused evaluation" is not a formal model or recipe. Nevertheless, he did provide concrete examples of procedures he had found useful in working "actively, reactively, adaptively" with identified decision-makers and information users on the program and agency policy levels.

The decision-theoretic approach advocated by Edwards, Guttentag, and Snapper (1975) involves participation by a wide range of decision-makers in both planning and evaluation. They reported use of this approach in developing an Office of Child Development research plan and in evaluating a Career Education Project.

Menges (1978) proposed a two-step process for "consultative participation" of program, legislative staff, and agency policy representatives with evaluators. This proposed process, however, is limited to the end of the evaluation—the time when interpretive judgment must be made—rather than to the design and implementation phase.

The U.S. General Accounting Office has issued a report to Congress called "Finding Out How Program Are Working: Suggestions for Congressional Oversight" (November 22, 1977: ii), which provides guidance for an interactive process that could be used for planning and carrying out congressional oversight of programs.

The six-element process begins when Congress enacts legislation authorizing a program. At that time oversight requirements are spelled out so that agencies know "what it is they are to report to the Congress, and when, about the implementation and evaluation of the program" (p ii). Elements 2 through 5 involve a series of reports by agencies, feedback from the congressional committee(s), and clarification/adjustment as necessary on executive branch policy, agency program design, program operation model, and planned evaluation measures. Element 6 is reporting the results of completed evaluation studies. This oversight procedure would establish a disciplined review process. Yet it permits "case-by-case flexibility for tailoring the type of evaluation to the nature of the program of legislation under review" (p. ii) since evaluations result from a series of *discussions* between committees and agencies. Such a process is expected to lead to greater use by Congress of the evaluations thus produced.

WHEN TO DO IT?

Active involvement of decision-makers requires a time and resource commitment by them that is not present in the more common, "traditional" evaluations. Consequently, there is a need to be selective. As with other decisions, some assessment will have to be made of the costs of active involvement and the benefits of enhanced decision-making ability through use of evaluative data. For example, Congress may wish to use all the elements of the oversight process proposed by GAO only with the most crucial pieces of legislation, and take a less active role in certain others.

WHO SHOULD BE INVOLVED?

The processes described here do not involve nebulous "audiences"—they are real live people interacting with others, which means that management decisions have to be made regarding work assignments. For example, the oversight process probably cannot be successfully accomplished without some specific congressional staff person having the responsibility to relate to a designated agency person. There already exist in the executive branch a variety of offices of planning, research, evaluation, and/or analysis. The staff in those offices may be likely persons to facilitate such a process. The individuals may well change, but at least there should be a position with that specific responsibility.

Processes requiring extensive interaction have implications for the perennial question of "inside" vs. "outside" (i.e., inhouse vs. contract) evaluators. Especially in the case of the congressional oversight process, it may be more likely that inhouse staff will have the rapport and expertise to interact in these ways. The Davis-Salasin change agent approach, on the other hand, may be neutral with respect to that issue.

A major justification for choosing "outside" evaluators and, perhaps, minimizing contact between them and program or agency personnel has been the desire to assure *independence* of the evaluation. However, outside evaluators are not themselves bias-free. They are also likely to want either to prove or disprove the program. Their own agendas—for example, publishing results to enhance their professional status—may in fact be detrimental to *useful* results. And the need for future contracts makes them not dissimilar to an inhouse employee with respect to financial vulnerability. The need for independence is an important issue but one too complex to be solved in that simplistic a way.

Serious attention must be given to ways to obtain the usefulness benefits of an interactive process while avoiding bias, or the appearance of bias, in the evaluation findings.

Other Factors

Certain other factors are important to evaluation utilization but, in varying degrees, can be removed as obstacles to utilization through interaction between decision-makers and evaluators.

QUESTION APPROPRIATENESS

One can guarantee a low rate of utilization for evaluation information which answers questions no one is asking or about which nothing can be done. Perhaps the most common problem of this sort is producing outcome data relevant for a program termination, go/no-go, decision when the real need is, instead, for help in improving the program. It is clear that the best way—perhaps the only way—to avoid this problem is through direct involvement of the evaluators with the multiple audience for the evaluative data.

METHODOLOGY

There is a lack of consensus on the topic of the methodological quality of evaluations. Some writers feel that evaluations are not rigorous enough while others feel that some attempts at experimental rigor lead to the exclusion of alternative useful methodologies. Some cite poor methodology as a reason why evaluations are, and should be, seldom used. Others say methodological quality is virtually irrelevant to potential users. The safest conclusion may be to strive for a methodology most appropriate to the questions being asked, including multiple data collection and analysis techniques.

Interaction between evaluators and decision-makers helps by narrowing the "knowledge gap" as to what decision-makers can expect from the evaluation. For example, being informed, in the design stage, of the limitations of a survey study may lead to either a change in the questions being asked or a change in resource allocation and timing so as to conduct a more methodologically rigorous investigation.

DISSEMINATION/REPORTING ISSUES

Dissemination/reporting issues include questions of method and style (readability of report, verbal as well as written reporting, etc.). But perhaps the most crucial issue is timing. If a decision must be made by a certain date and the report is late, the usefulness for that purpose is certainly destroyed. Perhaps as important is the damage done to decision-makers' willingness to use evaluation data produced in the future by these or other evaluators.

Writers about evaluation, however, differ in the importance they attach to timeliness as a factor in utilization. And some opinions differ across time. For example, Carol Weiss in her recent writings emphasizes timeliness less than she once did. Differential importance of this factor, as well as others, can be traced to the use for which an evaluation is intended. For instrumental use to make a specific decision on a now-or-never basis, timeliness is crucial. For less specific uses, or issues that will continue to recur, timeliness may be less crucial. Different types of decisions also require different time frames. "Routine" decisions like annual budgets must follow a routine of timeliness, including certain decisions to be made each year. "Innovative decisions" like those on creation of new programs may need longer time frames to assess impact.

An interactive process between evaluators and decision-makers solves many of the dissemination/reporting problems. The interactive process itself provides a mechanism for reporting results verbally as well as in a written report. Being "in touch" all along enables the evaluator to be aware of the decision-maker's time frame in any decision deadlines. And the decision-maker is in a better position to know if there are timing problems in the progress of the evaluation.

APPENDIX: SYNTHESIS OF FINDINGS

The following synthesis is the findings which emerged from GAO's 1978 study. The evaluation criteria were extracted from these findings.

Definitions Of "Use"

Research utilization is an extraordinarily complex phenomenon. Yet it can be analyzed like any other social phenomenon through a process of conceptualizing variables, defining them, and operationalizing them in a research setting. And as with other phenomena, clear definitions are necessary to make possible communication on the topic. Without such clarity one cannot make sense out of the otherwise conflicting assessments of such things as the extent of program evaluation use and what factors seem associated with that use. For example, Caplan (1977) reported that the *extent* of research use is primarily a definitional matter—hinging on conceptualizations of "use" and "research."

Weiss (1978) has proposed several dimensions of social research use. While they are certainly not orthogonal dimensions—some users may be more likely than others to use research in a certain way, for example—they are distinctive aspects of use. Adapting and expanding that set specifically for program evaluations suggest the following seven considerations.

(1) What Evaluative Information Is Used?

Shall we consider use of individual program evaluations or, instead, a "package" of reports on related programs in a given issue area?

Rich (1977) suggested that "information is used in groups or clusters and should be analyzed [with respect to extent of use] from that point of view" (p. 200). Menges (1978) proposed a two-step process to make use of evaluation results. It involves "consultative participation" of program and legislative staff with the evaluation staff on, first, the interpretation of evaluation findings and, second, the action implications. But he emphasized that these discussions must start with a summary of the main findings of a *set* of technically valid evaluations relevant to particular policy or implementation issues.

The information used can differ in type as well as in the extent of aggregation over studies. Caplan and his associates (1975) recognized a distinction between *hard* knowledge—"research based, usually quantitative, and couched in scientific language"—and *soft* knowledge—"nonresearch based, qualitative, and couched in lay language" (p. 18). It was this soft information—the social science generalizations, concepts, and perspectives—that was most cited as used by the federal policy-makers they interviewed.

(2) To What Type of Use Is It Put?

Pelz (1978) has presented a matrix combining Caplan's two types of knowledge with three modes of use, suggesting that either type of information could be used in either of the three ways. The three modes of use are instrumental/engineering, conceptual/enlightenment, and symbolic/legitimative.

Discussion of the use of evaluative information usually has an implicit definition of use as a direct and instrumental application: one can identify a certain action taken as a result of the information. An example of an instrumental definition of use is seen in the assessment by Waller, Scanlon, Kemp, and Nalley (1978) of LEAA's Model Evaluation Program. To be defined as "use," three criteria had to be met: (a) intended and actual users claimed the information was useful, (b) users cited actual instances of using the evaluation information, and (c) there was evidence that the use cited was important to performance of the user's function. This type of use is what Rich (1977) called "knowledge for action" and Knorr (1977) labeled "decision-constitutive." Knorr's research was similar to that of many others in generally finding little evidence of this kind of use.

There is considerably more evidence for use in a conceptual way. Knorr (1977), for example, found substantial evidence of what she called decision-preparatory use, where evaluation results served as a base or "ground" for actual decisions to take place. Patton et al. (1977) also found few instances of immediate and concrete effect on specific decision and program activities. But they found frequent impact as a diffuse and gradual process of providing additional information to reduce the uncertainty experienced by decision-makers. This mode of use also corresponds to Rich's (1977) "knowledge for understanding." Weiss (1977) has described it as use "in reconceptualizing the character of policy issues or even redefining the policy arena . . . [it] may sensitize decisionmakers to new issues [or] . . . revise the way that a society think about issues" (p. 16). Hence, she suggested the term "enlightenment" as well for this type of use.

The third mode of use is what Knorr (1977) called symbolic. Some examples are use of knowledge to substitute for a decision, to legitimate a policy already implemented, or to provide political ammunition. The use of information in these cases is not to decide on specific actions or to supplement the framework of understanding out of which later decisions arise but to serve political expediency.

(3) By Whom Is It Used?

To be considered "successful" at being used, must a study be useful to decision-makers at *all* levels of government? Or is it sufficient to meet, for example, the needs of program managers?

Lynn (1978) identified two problems limiting the policy relevance of federally supported local research and development (R & D), a broader category of research of which program evaluation is a major subset. The first relates directly to the question of users. He concluded that "too little thought is given to the types of knowledge that will be most useful to the agency, to Congress, to third parties, or to supporting disciplines prior to the commissioning of research projects. Little attention is given to developing priorities for guiding project selection" (p. 21). Or, as he put it, "few, if any, criteria of relevance are applied" (p. 21).

Lynn recognized the complexities of the knowledge-into-policy process and that "many criteria are appropriate to assessing the relevance of social R & D to policy making" (p. 22). That is, he acknowledged that there could be no absolute criterion for policy relevance, that the choice "will depend on one's values and perceptions concerning the appropriate federal role in supporting social R & D" (p. 19). Nevertheless, he asserted that "criteria of relevance must be consciously applied in the formulation of social R & D agendas, before projects are selected and funded, if social R & D activities are to have coherence and purpose" (p. 22).

In other words, there is no one answer to the question of who evaluations should be useful to. But ideally there will be a comprehensive evaluation plan that represents conscious consideration of the needs of different users (perhaps including the general public—see Marvin, 1977) and some decision as to which needs will be met by individual components and by the total plan.

(4) By How Many People Is It Used?

The issue here has been aptly put by Weiss (1978): "Is one convinced reader who forcefully propounds the research and advocates a position based on it sufficient, or is some minimal penetration of the decision-making group required?" (p. 34).

(5) How Directly Is the Use Derived from the Information?

Assessing the impact of an evaluation report is similar to assessing the impact of any other phenomenon (see Cook and Campbell, 1976). There are "internal validity" problems of knowing if any policy or program changes result from the evaluation rather than from some concurrent event such as a change in political administration. There are "construct validity" problems of separating the effect of specific recommendations from that of simply calling attention to the program. And there are "external validity" problems of generalizing from one study to another regarding what factors seemed important to utilization.

(6) How Much Effect Is Needed Before Research Is Considered Used?

Weiss (1978) suggested two aspects of this question: the strength of the impact and the direction of the impact with respect to the evaluator's intent.

The strength of an impact can vary considerably, and researchers have differed in what they consider an adequate impact to constitute evidence of use. For example, one could demand that all recommendations be implemented, and some be implemented, or, perhaps, just that they be considered. Weiss (1978), for example, considered research used if "a decision maker *considers* [italics mine] the findings of a study or a group of related studies . . . the research may not affect the decision, but it does get a fair hearing" (p. 35). Cook and Pollard (1977) also considered as use "the serious discussion of results in debates about a particular project or program" (p. 161) regardless of the type of use that is ultimately made of the information.

The direction of impact may be different from that intended by the evaluators since differing attitudes and values lead to differing interpretations of the same information. For example, the evaluators may recommend improvement of certain ineffective elements of a program. Program managers may, in fact, try to use those criticisms to improve the program while opponents see those same criticisms as justifying abolishing the program entirely.

(7) How Immediate Is the Use?

Instrumental uses are more likely to occur immediately and conceptual uses to be more delayed, to be "slowly percolated into orientations toward decisions" (Weiss, 1978: 34). The greater frequency of conceptual uses may, then, help explain why, according to Davis and Salasin (1975), "the evidence of effective utilization of evaluation becomes much clearer if one maintains observation over a sufficiently extended period" (p. 622).

These seven dimensions of use should make it clear that the task of defining utilization is a complex one. Yet it cannot always be avoided. For example, one criterion for adequacy of an evaluation system is its success at producing use-relevant studies. How, then, does one define use in assessing the success of evaluation on that criterion?

Schmidt et al. (1977) in their discussion of the different "markets" for evaluation stressed a need for differing definitions of use. They suggested that federal evaluations serve three markets: individual consumer, program management, and policy. They also asserted that (1) the different evaluation markets have different success criteria and (2) each market has different levels of evidence of performance which can be demanded by different reviewers. For example, the program management market requires as a success criterion that action be taken by management on evaluation results to affect the program design, while for the individual consumer market, satisfaction is a sufficient success criterion.

The literature suggests that there is no absolute standard for adequate "use." Instead, different kinds of use are appropriate for different evaluations. The greatest need is for some conscious consideration of the kind of use intended for the various elements of a comprehensive evaluation plan. If the objectives for use of the evaluation findings are thus clarified, they can then be assessed both as to whether others accept that definition of usefulness and as to whether the evaluation system is successsful at reaching that criterion of use.

Other Major Factors

There is no shortage in the evaluation literature of lists of factors related to utilization. Each writer's list tends to overlap partially but not entirely with every other's. In fact, the tone of the writing often implies an attempt to see who can name the most factors possibly related to utilization. Some have tried, however, to move beyond the listing approach. For example, Patton et al. (1977) asserted that

> the issue at this time is not the search for a single formula of utilization success, nor the generation of ever-longer lists of possible factors affecting utilization. *The task for the present is to identify and define a few key variables that may make a major difference in a significant number of evaluation cases* (p. 142).

This synthesis has a similar orientation. Consequently, it is not intended to be comprehensive of every factor ever listed as important for utilization. But there are problems in aggregating comments on even what seem to be the key variables.

The problems in synthesizing these evaluation writings are the same as in any meta-analysis of data or theory. A "head count" approach could be used. That would involve simply counting how many times a factor is mentioned, assuming greater frequency equals greater importance. But that approach mechanistically gives equal weight regardless of quality of study, orientation of the writer, etc. And there are still subjective problems such as deciding whether two issues discussed in slightly different ways are actually "close enough" to be considered the same.

This synthesis proceeded in a different way. Out of reading, thinking, and discussing, a necessarily subjective and qualitative organization of the literature emerged. It appeared that the diverse factors identified in the literature as important to utilization could be grouped in the following ways:

    the political decision-making environment,

—organizational aspects of the management environment,

—commitment/involvement of decision-makers and evaluators,

—appropriateness of questions asked,

—methodology, and

—dissemination/reporting issues.

(1) Political Decision-Making Environment

"The traditional academic values of many social scientists lead them to want to be nonpolitical in their research. Yet they always want to affect government decisions. The evidence is that they cannot have it both ways" (Patton, 1978: 46). Patton's assertion comes not only from his general observations of the evaluation scene, but also from his empirical study (Patton et al., 1977) of the utilization of federal health evaluation research. In that study, only two factors emerged as significant for utilization: a political factor and a personal one (commitment/involvement of the decision-makers).

Patton's call for evaluators to recognize and work with, rather than try to ignore, the poltical context is shared by Weiss (1973). She described evaluation as "a rational enterprise that takes place in a political context" (p. 37). Evaluation can be useful only when the evaluator is senstive to three ways political considerations intrude:

(1) Policies and programs themselves are creatures of political decisions.
(2) Evaluation results have to enter into the political arena of decision-making, where evaluative evidence competes for attention with other factors that carry weight in the political process.
(3) Evaluation itself has a political stance, as expressed in such things as selection of programs to be evaluated and acceptance of program goals for testing effectiveness.

A similar concern that evaluators develop a better understanding of the political realities has been expressed by Abt (1976), Cox (1977), Guba (1975), and Knezo (1974).

A more specific concern with the problem of imprecision of congressional language, and the difficulty that presents for designing useful studies, has been expressed by Chelimsky (1977) and Knezo (1974). Abt (1976) also raised the issues of goal conflicts about the purposes of evaluation and communications failures regarding work to be done. Conflicting vested interests, including those of the evaluator, were stressed by Goldstein et al. (1978).

(2) Organizational Aspects

Environmental characteristics of the organization which is the potential user of evaluation findings and/or in which the evaluation function is administratively located have been considered in detail by Davis and

Salasin (1975), Davis et al. (1977), and Weiss (1973). They have identified several characteristics which may serve to limit the performance and use of evaluation.

Davis has proposed a set of seven factors, called A VICTORY, on which an organization can be assessed in order to estimate the probability that a change (e.g., use of evaluation) will occur. Those factors are:

OBLIGATION—felt need to do something about a problem;

IDEA—information relevant to taking steps to solve the problems;

VALUE—predecisions, beliefs, manners of operating, and characteristics of the program organization

ABILITY—capacities to carry out the solution: staff, funds, space, sanctions;

CIRCUMSTANCES—prevailing factors pressing for a detracting from certain actions;

TIMING—synchrony with other significant events;

RESISTANCES—both front stage and back stage concerns for loss if specific action is taken; and

YIELD—felt rewards, benefits to program participants and consumers alike.

Davis has proposed that evaluators consider a four-step change technique consisting of assessment on the above factors, definition of the goal of the planned change effort (e.g., desired impact of the evaluation), action to shift conditions among the critical factors to the extent necessary, and follow-through.

Weiss (1973) identified the following organizational constraints on evaluation:

(1) conflicting perceptions of evaluation purposes;

(2) evaluation's place within the organizational structure;

(3) relationship between evaluators and practitioners (role differences, etc.);

(4) staffing of evaluation (part-time staff and high turnover);

(5) characteristics of the program (goal clarity, etc.); and

(6) timing of the evaluation.

Other writers have been less systematic in considering the total organizational environment, but have referred to one or another aspect as being relevant to utilization. Wholey et al. (1970) identified organizational inertia as a major roadblock to utilization. Chelimsky (1977) reported a need for structural incentives for use of evaluation and better organization for evaluation. Knezo (1974) described a need for program evaluation to be better integrated into program management. Menges's (1978) case study would support Knezo's view since he felt that utilization was enhanced by having some of the same people involved in both policy-making and evolution. Agarwala-Rogers (1977) maintained that evaluation research is more likely to be utilized when the evaluator is an insider to the organization because the evaluation will then be seen as less threatening. Weiss (1977) concurred on the greater use, especially in direct application of research findings to solve a specific problem, of evaluation done in-house by an agency's own staff. In a similar vein, Drob (1978) and Riecken and Boruch (1974) refered to greater utilization by program managers of relatively centralized, rather than decentralized, programs because of a closer link between the evaluators and the decision-makers.

(3) Commitment/Involvement

A recurring theme both in empirical studies of evaluation use and in theoretical articles has been the importance of active involvement and personal commitment to use by one or more decision-makers.

Waller et al. (1978) and Scanlon and Waller (1978) described the success of the LEAA-funded Model Evaluation Program in producing evaluation information that was used by state and local officials in criminal justice agencies and planning agency management and staff. Their major finding was that utilization of evaluation is achieved when the decision-maker is actively involved in production of the evaluation and feels ownership of the final product. A survey of federal government decision-makers and evaluators involved with selected national health program evaluations showed a similar finding (Patton et al., 1977). (The decision-makers were mostly office directors, division heads, or bureau chiefs.) Respondents repeatedly pointed to what the authors called the "personal factor" as the single most important element in the utilization process. As they reported:

> Where the personal factor emerges, where some person takes direct, personal responsibility for getting the information to the right people, evaluations have an impact. Where the personal factor is absent, there is a marked absence of impact. Utilization is not simply determined by some configuration of abstract factors; it is determined in large part by real, live, caring human beings (p. 158).

Their study also indicated importance of the personal factor throughout the evaluation, not just at the stage where study findings are disseminated. "If decisionmakers have shown little interest in the study in its earlier stages, our data suggest that they are not likely to suddenly show an interest in using the findings at the end of the study" (p. 159).

Case studies of individual programs or issues have pointed to the same conclusion. The use of social science evaluations in decisions on equal educational opportunity in the early 1970s was attributed to a real desire and commitment to their use by people at the highest policy levels of HEW (Menges, 1978). Swisher (1978) reported that involvement of decision-makers and their staff throughout led to evaluation of a nutrition improvement program that was useful in rewriting federal legislation, developing agency guidelines, and helping service delivery people.

The importance of this factor of commitment/involvement was also stressed by government agency participants at the Mitre Corporation Symposium (Chelimsky, 1977):

> It was pointed out, over and over again, that the most important factor in assuring the use of evaluation findings was *not* the quality of the evaluation but the existence of a decisionmaker who wants and needs an evaluation and has committed himself to implementing its findings (p. 31).

Other writers who have stressed this factor include Cox (1977), Davis and Salasin (1975), Davis et al. (1977), and Van den Ban (1963). Those who have emphasized the need for involvement especially from the beginning of an evaluation, including the design stages, include Agarwala-Rogers (1977), Ball and Anderson (1977), and Riecken and Boruch (1974). Johnston (1978) also stressed interaction "from the very first." He advocated engagement of the evaluator with the relevant *multiple* audiences at three points: prior to designing the study, when perspectives and needs of the sponsor and other audiences are determined; before conducting the research, when data collection plans and decision-making reponses for different possible data alternates are discussed; and after data are obtained, when the interpretation and decision alternatives are considered. Johnston described each additional interpersonal engagement as "an investment in the ultimate utilization of the research" (p. 11). This process of interacting with the relevant actors is thought to influence decision-making both by assuring the correct research design and measurement specifications and by "the cultivation of audiences who will wait the answers that the research can yield" (p. 4).

Other writers have also considered *why* this involvement seems to facilitate use. Goldstein et al. (1978) cited methodological and design problems such as evaluating phantom projects, selecting meaningful comparison groups, and identifying relevant variables as reasons for nonutilization. But strategies involving "consulting, communicating, and generally becoming more congruent with the administrators and program staff" (p. 25) were suggested as ways to deal with those issues. Weiss (1971) also pointed out the benefits of involving administrators and program people in the evaluation process: "not only does their participation help in the definition of evaluation goals and the maintenance of study procedure, but it may change the image of evaluation from 'critical spying' to collaborative effort to understand and improve" (p. 141). Abt (1976) called for participation by intended evaluation users in the legislature and the executive branch in some of the planning of evaluations. He saw that as a way to give "a sense of control, a sense of power over things, and basically more sharing" (p. 322). As a result, the "knowledge gap"—the lack of knowledge by evaluators of the political context of decision-making and by decision-makers of what evaluation research can really do—would be reduced.

(4) Appropriateness of Questions Asked

The need to investigate questions that are program related, properly focused, and of interest to users has been stressed by Cox (1977), Goldstein et al. (1978), Patton (1978), Wholey (1970), and many others. But Guba (1975) has pointed out the difficulty in knowing which *are* the right questions. Lack of agreement on the purpose of evaluation makes that a difficult task, as do the discrepancies between plans and operations. In addition, the program may change so that the initial questions become outdated and irrelevant. Abt (1976) stressed the need for evaluations that are "decision-driven." By that he meant focusing on variables that can be manipulated, i.e., policy variables rather than context variables.

Many writers have also argued that evaluators look at more than just outcome variables. There is a need for process and implementation evaluation as well, so that the evaluation can be useful in improving and understanding the program (c.f. Goldstein et al., 1978; MITRE Conference, 1978; Weiss, 1971). Agarwala-Rogers (1977) has pointed out that such evaluations may be useful not only because they answer different, possibly more relevant, questions but also because they are less threatening to program managers.

(5) Methodology

There is a considerable lack of consensus on the extent to which methodological quality is relevant to utilization. Some writers called for general improvement in the methodological quality of evaluations, usually meaning more "rigorous" designs according to social science research standards (cf. Abt, 1976; Guba, 1975; and Wholey et al., 1970). Menges (1978) called for a specific improvement in methodologies to relate impact to practical data about what is really happening (type of implementation). Goldstein et al. (1978) recognized the problem of "lack of excellence" on the part of researchers, but also pointed out that "excessive attention to rigor and excellence in design may divert the researchers' attention from substantive purposes of their work and, consequently, render utilization of evaluation research findings problematic" (p. 24).

Cox's (1977) analysis from the perspective of a model of managerial behavior suggested that, for program managers, "evaluation data will be grist for the informational mill and will be evaluated more against the overall informational context than against canons of scientific merit" (p. 506). Patton et al.'s (1977) survey of federal agency decision-makers did not find methodological quality to be a major factor in determining use of evaluation data. "There is little in our data to suggest that improving the methodological quality in and of itself will have much effect on increasing the utilization of evaluation research" (p. 151).

On the other hand, Patton (1978) did stress the importance of using an appropriate methodology. By that he meant not necessarily one that would reach some social science standard of experimental rigor but one agreed upon through active participation of identified decision-makers and information users with the evaluators. As a result of that participation, decision-makers should be more likely to understand the strengths and weaknesses of the data, believe the data, and, consequently, use them. Patton's viewpoint is that "the researcher has no intrinsic rights to unilaterally make critical design and data collection decisions" (p. 202). Those decisions are not neutral, objective, or rational; they are political, subjective, and satisficing (i.e., searching for a satisfactory solution, as distinguished from maximizing or optimizing), and they are affected by the evaluator's own sociomethodological biases.

Chelimsky's (1977) symposium summary may help understand the differing assessments of the importance of methodology to utilization. She reported that evaluators and agency representatives approached the problems of evaluation very differently:

> Evaluators tended to speak of evaluation essentially in terms of the technical excellence of the research and of the consequent conclusiveness attributable to the evaluation findings; they approached the questions of both excellence

and conclusiveness in terms of the experimental design, and tended to assume that use of the findings was a function of the quality of the research rather than of something else. Agency people, on the other hand, talked more of relevance, timeliness, breadth of analysis and responsiveness than they did of excellence or conclusiveness. . . . The general sentiment was that purifying the methodology and increasing the statistical "hardness" of evaluations would neither increase the use of evaluation findings by agencies nor help to answer the policy questions posed by decisionmakers (p. 31).

(6) Dissemination/Reporting Issues

Dissemination does not equal utilization, in spite of the implied message by some that *if only* evaluators would write better reports their studies woud be used. Yet the way of reporting results does certainly play some part in the use of that information (cf., Davis et al., 1971; Goldstein et al., 1978). Cox (1977) acknowledged that a written report will usually be needed but asserted that for most managers the most effective communication will be verbal. He also stressed, as did Patton's respondents (1978), the need for periodic reporting rather than trying to come up with surprises at the end. Agarwala-Rogers (1977) shared Patton's concern that a report be readable to administrators but that multiple channels of communication be used, not just a written report. Swisher (1978) emphasized the need for information to be reported in the original frame of reference from which questions were phrased by potential users, rather than from the theoretical perspective in which they may have been useful to evaluators while designing and conducting the research.

A broader issue than just the communication medium or style of reporting a single study is the need for a general system or process for disseminating evaluation information both to the users directly relevant to a given study and to other, more distant, potential users (see Knezo, 1974; Riecken and Boruch, 1974; Wholey, 1970). A variety of linking mechanisms have been proposed—an agriculture extension model, linking people or programs on the agency staff, the evaluator as an active participant in "marketing" his or her findings, etc. (cf. Agarwala-Rogers, 1977; Ball and Anderson, 1977; Chelimsky, 1977; and Drob, 1978).

The literature contains different messages on the importance of timeliness of reports for their utilization. In the survey of decision-makers by Patton et al. (1977) timeliness did not emerge as an important factor. Yet writers have commonly stressed the importance of timely reports (for example, see Agarwala-Rogers, 1977). Guba (1975) felt utilization to be limited by the rapid pace of change in society which may make it impossible to be timely enough. Weiss in her early writings (1971, 1972) stressed the importance of timeliness. But her later position (1977) was that timing is not so important as she once thought it was—social problems do not go away. Drob (1978) expressed a similar thought in saying that the genius of a good R & D manager is "to choose problems important enough to still be there when the study is finished."

It may be that the difference in importance of timing depends on the kind of use to which evaluation findings will be put. That is, whether the use will be "instrumental," to effect a specific short-term decision, or "conceptual," as one more piece of information contributing to subsequent decisions in an area. What is important, then, is to be sure all participants in the study are in agreement on the needs in a given situation. Menges (1978), for example, agreed that major issues do seem to reemerge and thus program evaluation results may be useful "next time." Yet in some cases, he insisted, timing is crucial. He proposed that a decision be made about the evaluations for which timing is most important and a special effort be made to get those results on time. He concluded that "the more members of the federal evaluation staff are actively involved in decision-making, the more they can and will communicate the need for timely and predictable delivery of results to the contractors" (p. 65).

The involvement of decision-makers in the evaluation process may solve some of the timeliness problems in another way. Because of their involvement, they may have more information about how the evaluation is going even though a final report is not yet available. And they should be in a position to avoid the sudden news three weeks before the report is due that it will, unfortunately, be three months late.

REFERENCES

ABT, C. C. (1976) "The state of the art of program evaluation," in Congressional Research Service, Legislative Oversight and Program Evaluation. Washington, DC. Government Printing Office.

AGARWALA ROGERS, R. (1977) "Why is evaluation research not utilized?" in M. Guttentag (ed.) Evaluation Studies Review Annual (vol. 2). Beverly Hills, CA: Sage.

BALL, S. and S. B. ANDERSON (1977) "Dissemination, communication and utilization." Education and Urban Society 9: 451-470.

CAPLAN, N. (1977) "Social research and national policy: what gets used, by whom, for what purposes, and with what effects." in M. Guttentag (ed.) Evaluation Studies Review Annual (vol. 2). Beverly Hills, CA: Sage.

——— A. MORRISON and R. STAMBAUGH (1975) The Use of Social Science Knowledge in Policy Decisions at the National Level. Ann Arbor: Institute for Social Research, University of Michigan.

CHEMLIMSKY, E. [ed.] (1977) A Symposium on the Use of Evaluation by Federal Agencies (vol. 2). McLean, VA: MITRE Corporation.

COOK, T. D. and D. T. CAMPBELL (1976) "The design and conduct of quasi-experiments and true experiments in field settings," in M. D. Dunnette (ed.) Handbook of Industrial and Organizational Psychology. Chicgo: Rand McNally.

COOK, T. D. and W. E. POLLARD (1977) "Guidelines: how to recognize and avoid some common problems of mis-utilization of evaluation research findings." Evaluation 4: 161-164.

COX, G. B. "Managerial style: implications for the utilization of program evaluation information." Evaluation Q. 1: 499-508.

DAVIS, H. R. and S. E. SALASIN (1975) "The utilization of evaluation," in E. L. Struening and M. Guttentag (eds.) Handbook of Evaluation Research (vol. 1). Beverly Hills, CA: Sage.

DAVIS, H. R., C. WINDLE, and S. S. SHARFSTEIN (1977) "Developing guidelines for program evaluation capability in Community Mental Health Centers." Evaluation 4: 25-29.

DROB, J. (1978) Personal communication, August 11.

EDWARDS, W., M. GUTTENTAG, and K. SNAPPER (1975) "A decision-theoretic approach to evaluation research," in E. L. Struening and M. Guttentag (eds.) Handbook of Evaluation Research (vol. 1). Beverly Hills, CA: Sage.

GOLDSTEIN, M. S., A. C. MARCUS, and N. P. RAUSCH (1978) "The nonutilization of evaluation research." Pacific Soc. Rev. 21: 21-44.

GUBA, E. G. "Problems in utilizing the results of evaluation." J. of Research and Development in Education 8(3): 42-54.

JOHNSTON, J. (1978) "What we know about the researcher and research methods in evaluation." Presented at the meeting of the American Educational Research Association, Toronto, March 27.

KNEZO, G. J. (1974) Program Evaluation: Emerging Issues of Possible Legislative Concern Relating to the Conduct and Use of Education in the Congress and the Executive Branch. Washington, DC: Congressional Research Service.

KNORR, K. D. "Policymakers' use of social science knowledge: symbolic or instrumental? in C. H. Weiss (ed.) Using Social Research in Public Policy Making. Lexington, MA: Lexington Books.

LYNN, L. E., Jr. (1978) "The question of relevance," in L. E. Lynn, Jr. (ed.) Knowledge and Policy: The Uncertain Connection. Washington, DC: National Academy of Sciences.

MARVIN, K. (1977) "Issues in managing applied social research." Presented at Council for Applied Social Research, Washington, DC, March 3.

MENGES, C. C. (1978) Knowledge and Action: The Use of Social Science Evaluation in Decisions of Equal Educational Opportunity, 1970-73. Washington, DC: National Institute of Education.

PATTON, M. Q. (1978) Utilization-focused Evaluation. Beverly Hills, CA: Sage.

——— P. S. GRIMES, K. M. GUTHRIE, N. J. BRENNAN, B. C. FRENCH, and D. A. BLYTHE (1977) "In search of impact: an analysis of the utilization of federal health evaluation research," in C. H. Weiss (ed.) Using Social Research in Public Policy Making. Lexington, MA: Lexington Books.

PELZ, D. C. (1978) "Some expanded perspectives on use of social science in public policy," in J. M. Yinger and S. J. Cutler (eds.) Major Social Issues: A Multidisciplinary View. New York: Free Press.

Program Plan for the Lead Division Area Evaluation Guidelines and Methodology (1978). Washington, DC: General Accounting Office.

RICH, R. F. (1977) "Uses of social science information by federal bureaucrats: knowledge for action vs. knowledge for understanding," in C. H. Weiss (ed.) Using Social Research in Public Policy Making. Lexington, MA: Lexington Books.

RIECKEN, H. W. and R. F. BORUCH (1974) Social Experimentation: A Method for Planning and Evaluating Social Intervention. New York: Academic Press.

SCANLON, J. and J. WALLER (1978) "Program evaluation and better federal programs." Presented at the meeting of the American Political Science Association, Phoenix.

SCHMIDT, R. E., P. HORST, J. W. SCANLON, and J. S. WHOLEY (1977) Serving the Federal Evaluation Market. Washington, DC: Urban Institute.

SWISHER, R. (1978) Personal communication, July 13.

VAN DEN BAN, A. W. (1963) "Utilization and publication of findings," in C. H. Backstrom and G. D. Hursh (eds.) Survey Research Methods in Developing Nations. Chicago: Northwestern University Press.

WALLER, J. D., J. W. SCANLON, D. M. KEMP, and P. G. NALLEY (1978) Developing Useful Evaluation Capability: Lessons from the Model Evaluation Program. Washington, DC: Urban Institute.

WEISS, C. II. (1978) "Improving the linkage between social research and public policy," in L. E. Lynn, Jr. (ed.) Knowledge and Policy: The Uncertain Connection. Washington, DC: National Academy of Sciences.

——— [ed.] (1977) Using Social Research in Public Policy Making. Lexington, MA: Lexington Books.

——— (1973) "Where politics and evaluation meet." Evaluation 1(3): 37-45.

——— (1972) Evaluation Research: Methods of Assessing Program Effectiveness. Englewood Cliffs, NJ: Prentice-Hall.

——— (1971) "Utilization of evaluation: toward comparative study," in F. G. Caro (ed.) Readings in Evaluation Research. New York: Russell Sage Foundation.

——— and M. J. BUCAVALAS (1977) "The challenge of social research to decision making," in C. H. Weiss (ed.) Using Social Research in Public Policy Making. Lexington, MA: Lexington Books.

WHOLEY, J. S., J. W. SCANLON, H. B. DUFFY, J. S. FUKUMOTO, and L. M. VOGT (1970) Federal Evaluation Policy. Washington, DC: Urban Institute.

Joseph F. Coates
Office of Technology Assessment,
Congress of the United States

5

IMPACT STATEMENTS IN THE
AUTHORIZATION OF LEGISLATION

"Irrational" is the vulgar canard most frequently leveled at the deliberations and actions of the U.S. Congress. This gross error reinforces the alienation of the ignorant. It also provides a ready escape hatch for those too indifferent to take the trouble to understand the process and how to effectively intervene, influence, use, correct, or reform the present congressional system. The rationality of the congressional process and its participants is total, multilevel, complex, subtle, and not fully public.

This chapter deals with a current attempt by the U.S. Senate to improve the quality of legislation by systematically anticipating the impacts of legislation. In February 1977 during the debate over reorganizing the Senate committee system, an amendment initially sponsored by Senator Talmadge, and modified somewhat by the then Senator McIntyre, was adopted. This was added as Section 5 of Rule 29 of the Standing Rules of the Senate, and effectively became a requirement for the conduct of senatorial business. Specifically, Rule 29.5 requires that every Senate committee, except Appropriations, include a regulatory impact statement as part of its report on legislation. The four key phrases in the requirements are: number of individuals affected, economic impacts, privacy, additional paperwork. The report is to accompany the bill as it leaves the committee, that is, as the basic work on the bill's formulation has been completed and it moves to consideration by the full Senate.

AUTHOR'S NOTE: *This chapter is drawn from "Anticipating the Impacts of Legislation: Implementing Senate Rule 29.5 Requiring Regulatory Impact Statements," by Joseph F. Coates and Betsy Amin-Arsala, Exploratory Group Staff Paper, Office of Technology Assessment, U.S. Congress, June 1, 1979.*

This reform originated in two ways. Senator McIntyre had been a member of the Commission on Federal Paperwork, which highlighted the congressional contribution to excessive paperwork. Independently, Senator Talmadge was expressing a growing concern about poorly framed legislation in general. The possibility of tying impact statements to legislation was also in the air as a logical extrapolation of the widely discussed environmental impact statements and the dozen other categorical impact statements required by, or considered in, other legislation. Although Senators Ribicoff and Magnuson expressed misgivings about its feasibility as a part of the legislative process, the rule passed by a vote of 74 to 20. Following this auspicious launching, the rule was almost completely ignored. While the Congressional Research Service had been called upon to examine the preparation of the statements, and prepared one draft impact statement to illustrate how they might be constructed, little happened by way of substantive use. Senator Chiles, from his position on the Governmental Affairs Committee, has become a champion of Rule 29.5. He commissioned a Congressional Research Service review of the extent of the implementation of the rule, and discovered that after two years 216 of the 688 committee reports which fell under its scope simply ignored the rule. Ninety percent of the rest gave reports one page or less in length, and many of the statements omitted one or more of the assessments required. Together with Senators Bentsen, Nunn, and Huddleston, Senator Chiles issued a "Dear Colleague" letter on January 18, 1979 to all Senators, urging them to join in monitoring future committee reports to insure compliance.

Meanwhile, several months earlier, September 19, 1978, Senator Harrison Williams approached the Office of Technology Assessment requesting assistance in implementing Rule 29.5. Reflecting his chairmanship of the Committee on Labor and Human Resources, Senator Williams highlighted the more specific needs of this committee under Rule 29.5. His committee is responsible for some $70 billion of congressional authorization, much of which is reauthorized annually. In May 1978 the committee reported 21 different bills in order to meet the deadlines imposed by the Congressional Budget Act. Additionally, over the horizon is the implementation of some form of sunset legislation, which will create additional demands on an already strained committee system. There is also a pressing need for the committee to have more effective tools to better cope with the budgetary and appropriations process. Moreover, there are special areas where the efficacy and the consequence of alternative legislation remain wide open in terms of opportunities, but clearly are uncertain in outcome, such as problems concerned with alcohol, drug abuse, and the education of handicapped children.

There is an acute awareness of the poor understanding by committees of the implementation of legislation by the federal agencies. Basically, the question is why well-intended laws often lead to overregulation, and in some cases to situations which thwart the intent of the law.

Senator Talmadge's Agricultural Committee, taking a dose of his medicine, prepared a Rule 29.5 report which was quite wide in scope. Since it was an ad hoc report on a specific bill, it was not a readily generalizable model.

The rest of this paper summarizes an attempt within the Office of Technology Assessment to assist in the implementation of Rule 29.5 by working out a systematic, practical plan for its implementation by committees.

The plan proposed is simple in that it requires the preparation and the utilization of systematic checklists with regard to the major components of Rule 29.5. Before going into some of the details of the checklists, it is useful to consider the benefits implicit in Rule 29.5 as a process for making legislation more rational, and then to turn to a set of alleged or putative constraints raised in background interviews with nearly three dozen people in the course of preparation of the plan.

BENEFITS OF RULE 29.5

The primary opportunity in Rule 29.5 is as a means of improving the legislative process by developing more explicit and detailed anticipations of beneficial and adverse effects on the American people and the economy, in time to permit consideration of alternative legislation or corrective instruments. One cannot expect perfection, but one can expect implementation to improve the legislative process. Implementing 29.5 also presents the opportunity to impact on the planning of congressional committees by encouraging the use of assessment tools more naturally and generally in their everyday business.

In meeting these primary objectives, other useful outcomes could be to:

— better integrate the committee's legislative proposals into the overall senatorial and congressional budget appropriations cycle;
— sensitize members and staff to the importance of secondary or unanticipated legislature effects;
— help clarify legislative intent by improving the record, and thereby providing possible guidelines for program monitoring and subsequent evaluations;

— promote the formalization and more general application of cost-benefit and other evaluation procedures by Congress;
— raise to new levels of quality the backup material accompanying Administration bills;
— improve hearings;
— facilitate the implementation of sunset-type legislation, should it be passed; and
— improve regulation.

DIFFICULTIES IN IMPLEMENTING RULE 29.5

Well over a dozen objectives, obstacles, and cautionaries have been noted by our contacts in regard to the implementation of the rule.

— Committees have a restricted number of staff who are already heavily burdened. There is general resistance to further expansion.
— Data collection relative to the regulatory impact reports would put potential adversaries, as well as supporters, on notice. That could be disastrous for current committee procedures.
— There is an intrinsic conflict between the intention of any bill and its impacts. Every bill must favor some interests over others, yet a systematic look at impacts will show those impacts on adversely affected parties and thus add fuel to the legislative controversy.
— If the burden of preparing regulatory impact reports were placed on committee staff, there would be a strong tendency to either respond in a pro forma manner or to hire out the assessment to a congressional agency. In either case, the staff members would benefit little from compliance since they could not be directly involved in the process.
— Insofar as the impact reports are not simply ignored, or become a mere pro forma step, they will influence the political processes in committees. The degree to which impact reports are effective would encourage their politicization. Those in favor of a new piece of legislation might force the use of data favorable to that position and restrict or suppress adverse information. In either case, the result would be an impact report of little value.
— The rule might do nothing more than create a paperwork burden for the committee staffs.
— The absence of clear and definitive consensual goals is characteristic of the present legislative and executive processes. In the absence of these anchor points, it is not likely that Rule 29.5 could have a primary impact on legislative intent or actions.

— The absence of specific definitions creates problems independent of the lack of goals. For example, we have no national consensus or definition of what a city is, much less what a city should be. Consequently, such things as urban-related programs are subject to a tremendous range of uncertainty.

— The Rule's possible use as an obstructionist device is unclear.

— Many argue that any impact process conducted by a committee or by committee staff must, by its nature, be superifical for two separate reasons. First, size and available funding limits what can be done. Second, the general orientation of committees is toward pushing legislation forward, and hence their role as primary advocates undercuts the willingness to probe unwelcome news in impacts.

— One alternative to the committees doing the bulk of the assessment is to go to the affected executive branch agency for evaluation. As the dominant evaluation mechanism, that could be defective in that it would rely upon part of the problem of the solution.

While there is merit to many of the obstacles cited above, it is not preordained that they will prevail. Rule 29.5, as a strategy to improve awareness of the implications of legislation, is a credible step forward. It seems likely that significant but incremental steps can be taken toward its full implementation.

THE CHECKLIST

Reflecting the goals, benefits, and cautionaries raised with regard to Rule 29.5, the tool which would have the widest applicability, as well as the greatest potential effectiveness, if specifically designed for each committee, is the checklist. Checklists would serve five functions:

— Be the framework for the reports required by the rule.

— Inform, suggest, and stimulate systematic attention and concern among staff and members about implications of legislation.

— Be the instrument for raising questions with the mission agencies. The agencies could be asked to respond to the complete checklist, or to prescribed items. Eventually this could establish the response to such questions as the necessary part of the executive branch submission.

— Provide the basis for more incisive hearings. Since all major legislation is likely to involve hearings, they could be used to raise questions with those who will be giving testimony, and to raise follow-on questions, particularly requiring supplementary materials from agencies or other institutional witnesses.

— Provide the framework for the evaluation of material offered by the agencies, either directly or in response to questions;

Completing the checklist are several other assessment resources:

THE CONGRESSIONAL SUPPORT AGENCIES

As one might very well imagine, the support agencies (the Congressional Budget Office, the General Accounting Office, the Congressional Research Service, and the Office of Technology Assessment) all have excellent reasons for not wishing to undertake routine work on Rule 29.5. Each of these agencies finds itself already working at the limits of its capacity. Therefore, a new task would require expansion into new topics, more staff, or the deferral of other activities. Furthermore, the agencies have no particular desire to routinely undertake work which, from every point of view, would be most effectively done by committees. The Congressional Budget Office already prepares a number of reports which relate to economic impacts, but they deal basically with budget implications for the government and inflationary effects, and do not cover the full range of economic effects as described below. The General Accounting Office undertook a limited effort similar to the OTA activity, not available at the time of this writing, which also attempts to develop a checklist strategy. The CRS has done a couple of stock-taking activities, and the one trial run mentioned earlier, but nothing further as far as we have been able to determine. Nevertheless, committees could acquire certain services from the support agencies on a routine or episodic basis including:

— preparation of detailed committee and subcommittee specific checklists expanding the general checklists already developed;
— Preparation of background material such as the systems maps discussed below;
— preparation of impact reports or elements thereof; and
— systematic review of agency and other submissions in response to Rule 29.5.

CENSUS BUREAU

The questions of the numbers, times, type, and distribution of individuals and businesses affected by any legislation could probably be handled swiftly, to a useful but rough approximation, by the Census Bureau's Data Users Service Division.

SPECIAL MEASURES

Other special tools and techniques could be brought to bear by the committee staff on an as needed, nonroutine basis, such as commissioning specific studies through contracts, workshops, and surveys.

FULL-TIME SPECIALIST

Hiring one or two full-time specialists on a trial basis, who have a suitable breadth of skills and interest to attempt the implementation of the above alternatives, could be worth a trial.

When to Prepare the Impact Report

The question of when to initiate the impact evaluation is not by any means trivial. In a typical legislative cycle (the 94th Congress in 1975-1977), 24,283 measures are introduced with about 12% of these (2,870) reported out of committee (588 became public laws). Committee staff are fully capable of recognizing quite early in the legislative cycle which bills are likely to come out of the committee and which bills are likely to be important. The question then becomes less one of selecting the bill than of orchestrating its evaluation. Ideally, one would want the impact preparation process to influence the structure of the bill. The bill, however, may change drastically during committee deliberations. Consequently, how does one allocate repeated investments in the assessments, and how does one orchestrate them in a way to give a positive effect? It would be useful if the bill to be reported out showed the comparative benefits and dis-benefits of its various alternatives as modified during deliberations. That may not be politically or administratively practical.

DEFINING THE SYSTEM

The Committee on Labor and Human Resources is responsible for a dozen or more major areas of American society from a senatorial point of view—labor, the handicapped, education, the arts and the humanities, employment, poverty, migratory labor, aging, health, scientific research, child and human development, alcoholism, and drug abuse. Consequently, in order to make a checklist a useful tool, one would have to develop for each area of the committee's interest a specific, systematic picture or map of the structure of that sector. For example, in the area of alcoholism, one would want to begin by diagraming in a flow chart the complete alcohol/alcoholism system in order to identify the stakeholders, the possible points of legislative effects and side effects, the economic elements in each of the steps along the way, and possible subtle points of secondary effects. The definition of each of these systems would be a basic contribution to the work of the committees or subcommittees, and would provide the conceptual framework for checklist development. No adequate systems description has been worked out for any of these areas. We see their initial working out then as part of an evolutionary process.

APPROACHING THE SPECIFIC REQUIREMENTS
OF RULE 29.5

Identifying the Numbers and Kinds of
Businesses and Individuals Affected

The qualitative identification of impacted individuals and businesses would obviously include the targets of the legislation, whether these are people in specific businesses, students, the handicapped, the aged, or whoever. Additional stakeholders, including some in opposition to a particular bill, would be brought out in hearings and in the normal collection of background material. The key qualitative problem is identifying those indirectly affected, those accidently affected, and those unintentionally affected. We see as useful a general checklist of types of businesses and individuals, complemented by a specific list reflecting each subcommittee's interest.

The initial assemblage of lists would be by combination of common sense and an examination of the affiliations of witnesses in past committee and subcommittee hearings. One could also develop further clues to identifying other stakeholders in terms of systems maps, mentioned above.

The quantitative identification of the number and types affected would result from turning to other information resources for numerical estimates. Cognizant executive branch agencies will undoubtedly have some population data on target individuals and businesses. A general resource in this regard is the Census Bureau's Data Users Service Division through a system of networking with the Bureau of Labor Statistics, the Social Security Administration, and other big data collectors. The Census Bureau could play a primary role in making and assembling estimates of the number of businesses and individuals affected. This module of the work seems straightforward, doable, and subject to steady improvement.

Approaching the Paperwork Burden

Paperwork is important for several reasons:

— Paperwork, and its electronic surrogates, are at the root of many of the privacy issues, which involve the misuse of information.
— Paperwork is the lifeblood of regulation, administration, and evaluation.
— Paperwork has created at least three kinds of adverse concerns: economic waste, psychological distress, and continuing abuse.

The Commission on Federal Paperwork summarized its observations on the role of Congress as follows: "Legislation is at the root of paperwork; consequently, paperwork reform requires the active support and participation of the Congress." The commission proposed, among other actions, that "the requirement for a paperwork assessment of new legislation is a useful technique." The commission, which made some 130 recommendations for reducing that burden, and a General Accounting Office study in 1978 on the paperwork burden placed on American businesses by federal agencies, form a solid basis on which to build a checklist.

A paperwork checklist must address seven general questions:

— who will generate what information, when, where?
— what will it cost?
— what is the purpose of the information?
— to whom will this be directed?
— how will it be stored, accessed, and distributed?
— what will be the secondary uses? and
— how will the paperwork process be initiated, evaluated, and terminated?

In order to go usefully beyond these general questions, a description of the paperwork burden cycle is suggested in Figure 1, and developed in more detail in Table 1. The Figure and Table suggest the organizational points at which a paperwork burden will arise. They would have to be expanded to include the specific needs of the individual committees. To get at the paperwork burden in more detail, a checklist of diagnostic questions is given in Table 2. An expanded portion of the checklist, dealing with costs taken from the commission's work, is shown in Table 3. These tables are only starting points and should be tested, evaluated, expanded, and modified to fit each committee's and subcommittee's needs. Even these simple tables point up the great complexity in systematically probing for normally unanticipated effects.

(Text continued on page 91)

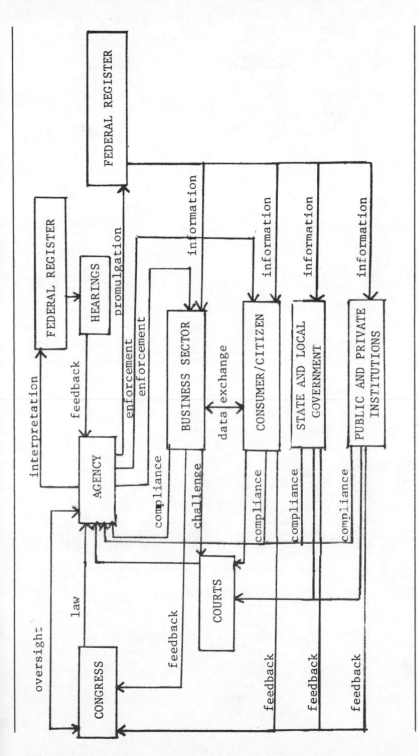

Figure 1: Paperwork Burden Cycle

89

Table 1: Paperwork Burden: A Checklist

A. Burden on Congress

    o   Preparation of a Bill

    o   Committee Debate

        − background preparation
        − hearing solicitations
        − preparation of impact statements
           regulatory
           cost estimates
           inflation

    o   Proper wording

    o   Associated correspondence

B. Burden on Federal Agencies

    o   Preparation of Proposed Legislation

        − data input to committee work
        − hearing testimony preparation
        − formal response to committee requests for review of proposed measures

    o   Interpretation of a Law

        − translation of notions and provisions of law into agency terminology
        − expression of gist of laws in regulation format
        − notification to affected parties of impending promulgation
        − hearings
        − impact statements
        − publication

    o   Implementation

        − contact/notification/instructions to compliers; frequency
        − monitoring reports; training new personnel for this job
        − self-reports by affected parties
        − processing of required personnel
        − paper cost to coordinate shared data with other agencies
        − ensuring specificity of program objectives to avoid over-collection of data

    o   Enforcement

        − training enforcement personnel; spot checking
        − processing violators
        − litigation and other legal costs

    o   Evaluation, Analysis, Surveys, etc., Over the Long-Term

        − collection of additional data for program assessment
        − provisions for periodic review and updating of regulation

Table 1 — Continued

C. Burden on Private Sector

   o Explanation

      — interpretation/education, in-house
      — general communication with relevant agency

   o Compliance

      — sequenced reporting to relevant agency
      — internal bookkeeping and accounting required to maintain proper data

   o Response to Agency Requirements; Simple, Complicated, One-Time, or Periodic

   o Solicit Assistance from Third Party in Order to Meet Stipulations, For Example, Lawyers, Tax Consultants

   o Bookkeeping

   o Number of Individuals Affected

D. Burden on Consumer/Citizen

    Ibid, See C.

E. Burden on State and Local Government

    Ibid, See C.

F. Burden on Educational, Health Care, and Other Institutions

    Ibid, See C.

Approaching Privacy

Approaching the privacy impacts was much more complex than paperwork, even in defining a checklist.

There is no clear, generally agreed upon definition of privacy since its constitutional concerns are in the 1st, 4th, 5th, 9th, and 14th amendments. The concerns about privacy are still growing. The collection, maintenance, use, and dissemination of information of a fairly conventional sort, coupled with development of new technologies for computers and telecommunications, is modifying the size, distribution, accessibility, and organizational arrangements for data use. So the technical aspects driving privacy concerns are in flux. Scientific and technological developments add further complexity to the matter. Such developments are going apace in many fields creating new or newly important potential privacy violations, such as advanced polygraphs, sensing devices, psychological tests, voice printers, blood and breath sample analyzers, eavesdropping and surveillance techniques, and telephone and wiretapping equipment. Even in the range of the interests of the Senate Committee on Labor and Human Resources, continuing new developments are raising fresh questions about altering human behavior, sterilization, lobotomies, mind control measures, and medical experimentation on institutionalized citizens such as the mentally ill and the military.

Table 2: Paperwork Burden Diagnostic Checklist*

A. Scoping Questions

Does the legislation require, encourage, permit, or suggest:

1. statistical formulas to allocate funding, benefits, services and assistance;

2. applications to Federal agencies;

3. government publications;

4. public disclosure;

5. privacy/confidentiality requirements;

6. Federal agency reports to the Congress;

7. reports from one agency to another (interagency reports);

8. reports from one non-government source to another;

9. unduly severe time limitations on the development and testing of regulations;

10. reporting dates or frequency;

11. records retention requirements;

12. standard setting;

13. program evaluations;

14. surveys;

15. plans;

16. granting the agency power to collect "such information as may be deemed necessary to enforce . . . ";

17. Federal agency reports from the public ("public-use" reports);

18. certifications and assurances;

19. eligibility criteria;

20. recordkeeping requirements, whether or not information physically flows to government.

---

*The items under A are taken from draft materials prepared by W. Buhler, formerly of the Commission on Federal Paperwork; Items under B are OTA generated.

Table 2 — Continued

B. Detailed Questions, if the Answer to Any of the Items Under A. is Yes.

1. Why is the information being collected?

2. Are copies or multiple forms required? Why?

3. Will the required data be available? How do you know?

4. What will it cost to generate, process, handle, and deliver? See **Table 4: VIII.**

5. Can the new information be acquired by using established forms, or their modification? By combining forms?

6. Are there exemptions to filing requirements? Why? Why not?

7. Are these data available elsewhere? How do you know? What is its quality?

8. At what frequency will information be collected? Why?

9. Is sampling appropriate, rather than universal data collection? Why not?

10. Are alternatives to paper permissible, practical, useable?

11. Will responses be machine readable? Why? Why not?

12. What would be lost if this data were not collected?

13. What is gained by collecting this data?

14. What are the total systems costs for collection? Specify the system's components and answer by system components. Use a flow diagram for clarity.

15. Will this information collection be pilot tested?

16. What models for parallel collections are available from which to draw lessons? How did you find them?

17. What are the alternatives to this means of data collection in acquiring the specified information?

18. What discretion will respondents have? How will they know that they have that discretion?

19. Who will design the forms? What guidebooks, guidelines, will be used?

20. How will the respondents be informed of specific and general, immediate and follow on use of the data?

21. Has this form a fog index? Who calculated it? When? What modifications could be made to lower the fog index?

22. Will this information collection reduce, eliminate, or replace an earlier collection? Why? Why not?

23. What specific channels at what level will be available for complaints about this form? How will the respondent know of that channel? How will they know that their complaints have been heard? Heeded?

24. How does this data collection relate to state, local, or private data collection needs?

25. Is any agency directly, or by implication, urged or required to collect or process information?

Table 3: Paperwork Costs Checklist*

1. first-time costs to design, develop and install information systems needed to furnish information requested by the government

2. repetitive direct and indirect costs of data collection, processing, and analysis

3. costs of filling out forms

4. costs to hire consultants, lawyers, accountants or other professionals to prepare reports

5. costs of time required to take part in the program

6. costs of program delays resulting from paperwork and red tape

7. costs to transmit or mail data

8. costs of correcting reporting errors on complex forms

9. personnel training costs

10. costs of time to understand what the government's requirements mean

11. costs of travel to government offices to discuss requirements

12. records/data storage costs

13. computer costs

14. overhead costs

15. costs of on-site government audits for data submitted

16. The number of people or organizations indirectly affected. For example, a requirement levied on States may require further surveys of local firms or individuals; or a requirement of Federal prime contractors may require them to collect information from sub-contractors.

17. Your ability to complete the information request. For example, a smaller business or community may have a harder time understanding the request and have less complete information systems from which data can be obtained than its larger counterpart. The expense of completing Federal reports may be proportionately more burdensome on smaller organizations.

18. The degree to which you are already burdened by other information requirements.

19. Any indirect burdens created by requirements that may invade your privacy, or may represent unwarranted interference.

20. The extent to which requirements concern information not formally kept for management purposes, may disrupt normal activities, or impose unrealistic deadlines which may affect the accuracy of the information provided.

Source: U.S. Commission of Federal Paperwork. *Paperwork Action Kit.* Washington, D.C.: Commission on Federal Paperwork 1977.

The limited approach we pursued in the preliminary analysis was to recognize the central role of information on privacy risks, and take that role as the basis for the beginning of a systematic diagnosis, as a model for other privacy areas. Fortunately, there have been a number of background

studies by academics, by the Privacy Protection Study Commission, the Commission on Federal Paperwork, the Electronic Funds Transfer Commission, and even nongovernmental groups such as the National Commission on Confidentiality of Health Records. As early as 1973, the Committee on Automated Personnel Data Systems of the U.S. Department of Health, Education and Welfare laid down some principles comprising a "code of fair information practices." There have been, in addition, ten major privacy-related acts between 1968 and 1978. There are also the "privacy impact statements" required under the privacy act of 1974, as implemented by the Office of Management and Budget. As an institutionalized impact requirement, such required analyses have been around long enough to have acquired a useful body of experience. The OMB, in examining proposals to establish or alter any system of record for its implications on privacy and other personal property rights of individuals, focuses on four key questions:

— the amount and nature of personnel data to be collected;
— what the system is to be used for;
— to whom records will be disclosed; and
— whether computers will be used, and if so, how they will be safeguarded against improper access.

Nevertheless, attempts to define a systematic approach to privacy impacts is in a primitive stage. A taxonomy of actual and potential threats and abuses to privacy has yet to be laid out. This taxonomy would deal with information flow, and with the other kinds of scientific and technological developments suggested above. Such a taxonomy would depend upon detailed estimations of the very nature of privacy and potential privacy violations via systematic inventory of acts, rules, regulations, legislation, agency practices, and so on. Identification of potential future technologies which might influence privacy would also be required.

We prepared a privacy checklist, similar in kind to the paperwork list, raising close to 100 questions (Table 4). Those 100 questions do not lend themselves to clear, crisp, instantaneous yes/no responses. Rather, they are diagnostic, suggesting that the answer to each requires some substantial study and analysis. No checklist by itself is worth anything unless it is backed by, or forces itself to be backed by, an adequate analytical effort such as that suggested above.

(Text continued on page 101)

Table 4: A Privacy Issues Checklist Relating to Information Systems

I. A. Does this legislation authorize, mandate, encourage, imply, or involve the establishment of an information collection system?

   B. See paperwork burden diagnostic checklist.

II. Purpose of the System

   A. For what is the information system to be used?

   B. Does the proposed information system relate to a reasonable authorized agency program in scope, breadth, and usability?

   C. Is the nature and amount of data to be collected appropriate for its intended users? How was this established? How will the data be used?

   D. To whom are records disseminated? Available? Under what legal, administrative, and procedural safeguards?

   E. Will computer networks and ADP be used? What are the safeguard issues, and how will safeguards be developed, listed, and evaluated?

   F. What are the alternatives to the information system, proposed or implied?

III. Social and Political Implications

   A. Is the proposed information collection consistent with a free society? With existing legislation?

   B. What is new or unique about the capacity or potential of the system as a management support tool and as an operating mechanism? Is this a departure from current means?

   C. In those segments of the public and private sectors which are the subject of the legislative/regulatory policies, what trends and processes in relation to privacy could be accelerated, aggregated, improved, or set in motion by installing the new information system?

   D. What new groups will be brought more effectively into the regulatory system? Who are currently overlooked, ignored, under-represented, or under-serviced? Who benefits and who stands to lose?

   E. What relationships among institutions might be established and what current ones affected?

   F. What are the political implications, beneficial as well as adverse, of the new system for governmental control over the individual and over the general population?

   G. How could the system be used for the surveillance and monitoring of actions and behavior?

   H. To what extent, if any, might the system contribute to the growth of federal social control, or become an instrument for subversion of the democratic process?

   I. To what extent, if any, does the proposed system in combination with other federal systems in the Internal Revenue Service, Social Security, HEW, and other agencies expand the potential surveillance capacity of the federal government?

Table 4 — Continued

IV. Agency Missions

    A. Will the proposed system make it more difficult for some people to reintegrate into society and thus impede their rehabilitation?

    B. In what ways, desirable or undesirable, might the system cause, or contribute to, changes in the operation or organization of the agency and its clients?

    C. What is the likely impact of use of the system on caseloads?

V. Control and Accountability

    A. How can the Congress satisfy itself that the procedures initially proposed under the system are adequate with regard to security and confidentiality? What data, information, and monitoring are required to meet this oversight need?

    B. How can the Congress monitor the operations of the system in order to satisfy itself that new opportunities to breach security and confidentiality have not developed or been created within the system? What review of the system should be planned, at what stage, and how frequently?

    C. How could the new system affect committee oversight and chances of satisfactory accountability to Congress:
       (1) by the rest of the Executive Branch?
       (2) by governmental contractors and other users?

    D. How can agency review and evaluation be built in?

VI. Federalism

    A. How will the system affect the present federal/state relationships? Can or will the system be used directly or indirectly to assist state programs? Will development of the system promote initiatives to combine or share state and local systems?

VII. Private Sector

    A. How could the system or its future generations affect the relationships with private organizations, institutions, and businesses?

VIII. Implications for the Individual

    A. What could the new system mean for the potential of the agency and the rest of government to investigate the individual?

    B. What could the system, and its future generations, mean in terms of the individual's ability to start anew in society?

    C. How may the new system affect the individual's control over what personal and financial information is supplied to government and the person's participation in how it is shared, transferred, manipulated, and managed?

    D. How may the new system affect, for better or worse, the quality of service to the citizen? Will increased speed and efficiency in transfer and storage of information necessarily mean improvement in protection of privacy, relevance of data maintained, confidentiality, and accuracy and timeliness of records?

Table 4 — Continued

E. What problems of privacy are likely, or possible, to arise for the individual in light of new technological developments?

F. To what extent is it feasible for the individual to "purchase" varying levels of privacy in the system?

G. What are the costs of assuring various levels of privacy to the individual with respect to data bases held in both the public and private sectors?

H. To what extent would more stringent privacy requirements have a negative impact in terms of protecting other social goals?

I. In what ways might the individual gain access to information in his personal files to enable him to insist upon correction of errors? At what cost? To whom?

IX. Legal Implications

A. Which statutory standards, guarantees, and sanctions apply to the system?

B. If the new system is installed, are existing statutory standards, guarantees, and sanctions governing federal information policy adequate to safeguard:
(1) the privacy of the individual?
(2) the confidentiality of taxpayer information?
(3) the security of the system?
How were the responses to 1-3 determined?

C. How could changing concepts of privacy and constitutional rights in the courts and Congress affect the system? How was the response determined? What are the basic assumptions in the response? What legal remedies are available or should be considered to counter threats to privacy, security and integrity?

D. Will the proposed system strengthen trends towards administrative justice as opposed to traditional conceptions of legal due process, presumption of innocence, and full, fair, and open hearings?

E. What is the likely effect of the proposed system on the administrative process and relationships between criminal justice agencies?

X. Economic Implications

A. Does the system raise unexamined economic issues?

B. Could the system result in intensified regulation and increased control over the individual or organization, resulting in more coercion being applied with the possible consequence of reduction in the level of voluntary compliance?

C. Will there be a cost-benefit analysis involving factors other than those of cost and efficiency involving the social and political trade-offs?

XI. Administrative and Managerial Issues

A. Does the proposed system raise issues of need for administrative and management changes in overall processing methods?

Table 4 — Continued

    B. Does the proposed system raise issues concerning the tolerance of the administrative structure and manpower capacity of the agency to carry the load of technology involved? Can the system get too large, the data bank too unwieldy, for administrative purposes?

    C. What kinds of detailed management information does Congress need to know to evaluate the impact of the ADP system on individual and group privacy? Is there a need, for instance, to address such questions as:

        (1) How many employees are now involved?

        (2) How many more will be added?

    D. Does the system raise issues of the accountability of the administration of the programs as they may bear on the privacy and other rights of individuals to:

        (1) the Secretary or Administrative head?

        (2) the President?

    Will they be able to keep track of what other government agencies are doing with the data, how they are aggregating, manipulating, and sharing it?

    E. What issues are raised by any network feature of the system?

    F. How will proposed system relate administratively to other agency systems and to other governmental data banks and systems? Who could access it, feed it, retrieve from it?

    G. Does the system present issues of controlling abuses of authority by political administrators and management officials?

    H. Should these and other issues of administration and management be addressed in legislation as opposed to regulations?

    I. To what extent will PSI considerations spur or retard the program's objectives?

    J. Are the available oversight and auditing mechanisms strong enough to alert society to adverse consequences in time to avoid or reverse them? What are they?

XII. Technical Issues

    A. Do the size of the proposed system and its network features raise issues of the wisdom of it and its technical feasibility?

    B. Does the proposed system raise problems of guaranteeing sufficient technical safeguards for maintaining the integrity of citizen information and protecting it against unauthorized use?

        (1) Has sufficient attention been accorded those various components of information management which are necessary for the type of personal and business information contained in the new system including such matters as:

            (a) partitioning and segmenting of files,

            (b) data input, storage, handling,

            (c) record identification,

            (d) media control,

            (e) programming techniques for security,

            (f) software documentation,

            (g) data elements?

Table 4 — Continued

    (2) Has sufficient attention been accorded the establishment of technical guidelines and administrative regulations to govern computer system and network controls including such matters as:
      (a) user identification,
      (b) terminal identification,
      (c) data access controls,
      (d) data encryption,
      (e) security auditing?
    (3) Has sufficient attention been accorded needed aspects of physical security?

C. Has sufficient attention been accorded needed aspects of vulnerability to natural and man-made disasters, terrorism, planned disruption, or sabotage, and their effects?

D. Can "appropriate" levels of privacy, security, and integrity (PSI) be defined?

E. What are the technical and managerial approaches and likely costs of implementing various levels of PSI?

F. Is it feasible to offer different levels of PSI for the same service at different costs?

G. Should technical standards be required for safeguards? Who should, or could, set them—FCC, state and local authorities, the agency, OMB?

H. What problems of privacy, security, and vulnerability would arise in the expanding use of the system? Are there specific scale problems associated with the system?

I. Will services expand, making certain portions increasingly vulnerable?

J. If serious vulnerability does arise, who should have the responsibility in or outside government to design countermeasures?

K. What are these countermeasures likely to cost?

XIII. International

A. To what extent is the growth and handling involvement of international data bases likely to arise and pose problems?

B. What are the pros and cons of individual countries permitting the exportation of data bases only by government approval?

C. Is the emergence of data havens posing problems of security and privacy; if so, in what way?

D. What kinds of international agreements and national policies appear advisable to cope with these problems?

XIV. Research

A. What needs, requirements, or provisions are there for access to data for preparation of:
    (1) policy research?
    (2) program evaluation?
    (3) scholarly and academic research?
    (4) social indicators?

B. Will these uses be appropriate? Who will decide?

Table 4 — Continued

XV. Centralization/Decentralization Choices

    A. Is there a conflict between maintaining national privacy and civil liberties and centralizing/decentralizing implications of the system?

    B. What would be the impact of centralization/decentralization on the opportunity for oversight of constitutional rights protection throughout the country?

    C. Would it be more or less possible for interested groups to focus attention and violations or patterns of governmental abuses?

    D. Would a centralized/decentralized system be more or less responsive to the privacy concerns of individuals?

Approaching Economic Impacts

The economic impacts of regulation are now the subject of sweepingly critical, public, legislative, and executive concern. Getting at economic impacts presents a major conceptual and practical problem in the implementation of Rule 29.5. The very factors that make the anticipation of economic impacts important also confound the problem. What is a useful scope of economic effects? It is in the interest of many to have economic impacts narrowly defined. Highlighting only cost, for example, to a highly polluting industry to improve its processes, would work to its advantage. On the other hand, total social cost analysis of the failure to take more, rather than less stringent measures might work to its disadvantage. Second, it is not at all clear what are the practical limits of the attempt to get at impacts. Third, economic impacts are often highly distributed among regional areas, states, and localities, yet we have a better national data base for getting at aggregate effects. Counterposed against data discrepancies is the fact that the politically most active elements in society are those that are affected by the details, and hence the distributed economics have more political impact than the aggregate economics. Adding further complexity to this problem is that experts disagree—often because of differences in their assumptions about such critical factors as scope of effects, discount rates, and interest rates.

The expansion of regulation in the last two decades, reflecting the growth of new social policies and greater practical concerns for health, safety, and quality of life, have led to regulatory overresponses, and therefore to an impatience to correct those overresponses. It is obvious, therefore, that the institutional support structures, the analytical models, and the data bases to sustain adequate analyses in these new regulatory areas are deficient. Attempts within the executive branch to focus on inflationary consequences have not been fully adequate, partly because of required new learning intrinsic to that process, partly because of the obstacles listed above, and partly because of the furor often implicit in making clear and public any factors affecting the economy. Any economic news that is not unequivocally good tends to be a natural candidate for suppression.

Nevertheless, we did offer a preliminary checklist of factors that should enter into the definition of economic impacts which emphasizes: (a) the process steps required, such as identification of parties of interest, definition of the service delivery system, rough cut estimations of contributions of each of the sectors of the overall economy, etc; (b) a set of questions dealing with explicit direct and indirect costs to be covered, opportunity costs, transaction costs, transition costs, and steady state costs; (c) a roster of more specific questions; and (d) economic impacts reports should be prepared with both aggregate and distributive costs and benefits formatted, and the uncertainties associated with the numbers given greater prominence.

SUMMARY

All factors considered, the single most valuable tool for the committees in implementing Rule 29.5 would be systematic checklists of considerations affecting the four impact areas. Checklists would alert members and staff to some normally overlooked implications of legislation. Checklists could also be the basis for a strategy of raising questions with the executive branch agencies, and for framing questions for development during hearings. Checklists are also compatible with time and labor constraints on staff.

Charles C. McClintock
Cornell University

6

A PROGRAM REVIEW AND EVALUATION SYSTEM:
Framework for Congressional Committees

With the advent of sunset bills in the Congress and the passage of a variety of sunset acts in state legislatures, there is increasing need for examination of the interplay between legislative processes and program evaluation. Unrealistic expectations are likely to exist among the various parties associated with legislative program review and evaluation, including evaluation professionals, legislators and their staff, program staff, and the public at large (Kivens, 1978). A major need in this area is the development of systems for quantitatively based program review and evaluation that are suited to the oversight and decision processes of legislative committees and that are keyed to legal enactments of programs.

Reviews by Behn (1977) and de Leon (1978) of the prospects for automatic sunset program reviews represent sober analyses of the constraints imposed by all of the actors mentioned above on the legislative processes of evaluating, reauthorizing, or terminating public programs. Their pessimism regarding the possibilities for automatic program termination should not be viewed as negative with respect to the opportunity for careful legislative program review. For instance, Zweig's (1979) analysis of the trend toward a "managerial Congress" beginning with the Budget and Impoundment Control Act of 1974 (P. L. 93-344) indicates that a clear signal is being sent that, at least at the federal level, legislative program review and evaluation will incorporate more detailed, systematic, and replicable procedures than have been characteristic of the past. The reasons

AUTHOR'S NOTE: *I am grateful to Irving Lazar, Steven Maynard-Moody, and Elizabeth Reilinger for their criticisms of earlier drafts of this articles.*

for this are manifold and include concerns with fiscal and budgetary restraint, interbranch prerogatives (vis-à-vis the executive in particular), and a desire for a more complete record of information on program expenditures, activities, and effects in order to guide the investigative, authorizing, and appropriating processes of legislative committees. There are limits to the rational management capabilities of legislative bodies. Even though Weber (1958) viewed the legislature as the ultimate source of legitimacy and control over public bureaucracy, it also has critical symbolic and compromise functions for the competing desires and values of societal interest groups. Often some of the desirable features of policy and program evaluation, such as clearly defined objectives, are not present in authorizing legislation since its enactment depends on deliberately vague or ambiguous language that will satisfy contradictory demands from different constituencies.

Still, legislatures at state (Crane, 1977) and federal levels (Beckman, 1977) are developing greater capabilities for policy analysis that will support legislative oversight and decision-making processes. This is due on one hand to a desire to recapture decision-making responsibility from the executive agencies that implement legislation and on the other hand to the need for defensive strategies when enacting policies that are unpopular, especially reductions in appropriations. While political compromise continues to be the dominant mode of dealing with conflict, technical analysis with its ideals of objectivity can also assist the legislator in openly making choices that involve adverse affects for certain groups.

As Bunker (1978) has argued, the processes of science and politics can interact in a jointly corrective manner to the overall improvement of policy making. The realities of political life force the analyst to refine research methods and oversimplified causal models and to be concerned with matters of the utilization and impact of analysis in addition to its technical qualities. Similarly, the theories and methods of social science can enrich the perspectives of policy makers, in particular by objectively examining policy options and posing questions that may be politically dangerous. Also the discipline that comes from scientific analysis can correct the errors of superficial explanation and conventional wisdom that often characterize political posturing.[1]

The major purpose of this article is to develop a framework for designing a mechanism for legislative program review and evaluation. The structure and functions of this mechanism closely resemble a management information system for programs under the authorizing jurisdiction of a particular legislative committee. While a management information system is only one of several means for legislative oversight and control, it serves as a building block for grounding and interrelating various procedures and systems for program review and evaluation.

The following sections of this article describe (1) a general description of legislative program review and evaluation procedures; (2) some of the features, requirements, and performance expectations of a computer-based management information system for legislative committees; and (3) the boundaries of effectiveness for a legislative management information system.

PROGRAM REVIEW AND EVALUATION IN
THE CONTEXT OF LEGISLATIVE
OVERSIGHT AND CONTROL[2]

The term *program review and evaluation* is meant to convey a broader range of activities than is normally found in evaluation research. Review implies retrospective and prospective analysis including assessment of political, bureaucratic, fiscal, statutory, and budgetary features of programs and policy options. Evaluation is more focused and refers to studies of program efforts and outcomes in comparison to desired goals. The two processes overlap at many points and will not be systematically distinguished in this discussion.

Traditionally the terms *oversight* and *control* have had political or accounting connotations. For example, legislatures employed tactics such as special investigations, public hearings, legislated executive management procedures, audit agencies, patronage appointments, and threats and promises made to agency executives by individual legislators and their staff. While practices of administrative science became widespread in the executive branch, legislative committees had very little data or analytic capability that they could call their own. Thus, program evaluation was a limited option for oversight and control.

This situation has changed substantially with the growth of congressional agencies such as the Office of Technology Assessment, Congressional Budget Office, Congressional Research Service, and the General Accounting Office (Beckman, 1977) and their counterparts at state levels (Crane, 1977). These agencies can produce a great range of policy and program analysis for the Congress including fiscal and performance audits, legislative reviews, special studies and forecasts, evaluability assessments, and secondary analyses of program evaluations.

Problems with Current Approaches to Legislative Program Review and Evaluation.

There are three problems, however, with the approaches to program review and evaluation currently available to the Congress. First, committees must rely too heavily on data generated for agency purposes which are subject to the self-promotional interests of agencies and organized in formats that are most meaningful to the executive program and accounting structures. Second, even when analyses can be organized according to the programmatic and policy interests of the Congress, they may not be uniformly or comprehensively linked to information on authorizing legislation and appropriations levels. This makes it more difficult to translate findings from program review and evaluation into the specific decision requirements of the legislative process. Finally, without standardized information that is collected at regular intervals, there is little capacity for organizational memory and learning. Effective program review and evaluation requires some method of knowing what policies and programs have been tried, at what levels of effort, and with what effects. Without this basic information it is difficult to apply past experience to examine proposals for change or even to know the full range of current program efforts, given the fragmented information that is available on a large number of programs.[3]

A Legislative Management Information System

What is needed, in addition to the review and evaluation capabilities already available to the Congress, is a legislative management information system that is based on standardized units of analysis (in this case, programs) and that contains textual and numerical information on program budget, activity, evaluability, and evaluation status. Such a system would be computerized and supportive of the other program review and evaluation procedures of the Congress and of other techniques for legislative oversight and control. It would be keyed to authorizing legislation for all programs under a committee's jurisdiction thereby focusing legislative decisions on the specific sections of law pertaining to a particular program or category of activity.

The issues related to design and implementation of a computerized program review and evaluation system (abbreviated to PRES) are very similar to those that arise in a sample survey. The next section is organized around the phases and processes of a survey as a heuristic method for anticipating problems in PRES. Little systematic attention will be given to the possible agency structures for implementing PRES, to staffing for the kinds of analysis that could be done with PRES, or to modes of legislative and executive organization for dissemination and utilization of PRES outputs. These are critical issues but they deserve more attention than can be given here (see Comptroller General of the United States, 1977; Crane, 1977: ch. 2).

TECHNICAL AND
ORGANIZATIONAL FEATURES OF PRES

The U.S. Senate Committee on Labor and Human Resources has created procedures for budget review and oversight that serve as a basis for developing a broader computer-based program review and evaluation system.[4] Examples from the design and implementation of the committee's Budget Review System will be used throughout this section to illustrate features of PRES.

System Design

A PRES would be structured as a longitudinal census of a population consisting of all programs under the authorizing and appropriating jurisdiction of a committee. The number of waves of data collection would vary depending on which variables were being updated. For instance, budget data might be compiled on quarterly, annual, or biannual bases, while evaluation data might be reported on a sporadic basis as they became available. The virtue of the longitudinal design is that it yields trend data which permit descriptions of change and causal inference (Cook and Campbell, 1979: ch. 5). It would be possible, for example, to look at the effects of changes in authorizing language or appropriations levels on various indicators of program activity and performance.

There are enormous problems in attributing causality at such a broad level. Internal validity is threatened in several obvious ways. For example, changes in time series data may reflect historical trends rather than specific changes in legislative authorizations and appropriations. Second, the implementation of legislation by executive agencies creates major complications for causal analysis of legislative action. Administrative behavior at federal, state, and local levels is difficult to measure and sorting out the effects of changes in agency personnel and policy from legislative action may be impossible. Agency actions may contravene legislative intent, or they may provide the desired effects but not because they performed the activities called for in the legislation. Finally, it is difficult to find measures for the intended effects of legislation that are valid, sensitive enough to detect change, and politically viable.

At the least, given the large number of observations over time on many programs, there would be ample opportunity for inquiries regarding the causal effects of legislative action. The accumulation and comparison of separate analyses would aid the process of ruling out plausible alternative explanations for legislative impact. The problem of adequate indicators of program effectiveness is more intractable, however, and raises another complication. Longitudinal designs with many waves of data are particularly vulnerable to changes in instrumentation and measurement procedure over time and to the effects of missing data (Sonquist and Dunkelberg, 1977: ch. 2). The management of PRES must include sufficient resource allocation for trouble-shooting these data management problems.

A problem with longitudinal designs is that they involve more complex analyses than cross-sectional or control group studies (e.g., Cook and Campbell, 1979: ch. 6). This is especially true when one is attempting to make causal inferences about the effects of legislative changes as opposed to purely descriptive reviews of appropriations trends, for example. Analyses require procedures for separating the effects of periodicity and autocorrelation across time periods in order to detect change that can be attributed to specific authorizing or appropriating actions.

Despite these problems, a legislative committee needs to concern itself with causal inference as much as descriptive analysis. The justification for trying to determine causality need not be based on scientific curiosity which, in any event, would be insufficient grounds for legislative inquiry. Rather, the question for the legislative committee is, "What are the effects of our programmatic, budgetary, and fiscal decisions?" This pragmatic query represents a very complex set of causal questions that nonetheless mark the bottom line of accountability for the legislature.

Sampling and Units of Analysis

Sampling procedures could be instituted on a purposive or random probability basis to make various nonroutine estimates of special interest to a committee, for example, to determine increases in appropriations level or quality of evaluation data on selected programs. Purposive sampling might be of particular interest to the oversight responsibilities of a committee. Programs under specific implementing agencies could be sampled for purposes of performance comparisons over time. Similarly, if a committee's jurisdiction is broad enough, functional areas such as health care programs could be reviewed across the various agencies in which they are found including health, education, social services, and labor.

The issue of appropriate units of analysis is critical to the legislative utilization of PRES. The experience of the Committee on Labor and Human Resources in developing the Budget Review System is instructive on this point. The committee decided that for purposes of budgetary oversight and legislative review, the most meaningful unit of analysis was each major section of an act that was intended to implement the purposes of the authorizing legislation. These sections were called programs and they became the principal entities for data collection and analysis. When legislation was specific about the processes and forms that programs would take, subunits called activities (within programs) and projects (within activities and programs) were identified.[5] These definitions placed the focus of PRES analysis on the ultimate policy documents—the legislation that authorized the existence of a program.

DEFINING THE BOUNDARIES FOR UNITS OF ANALYSES

There are several problems that arise when these units of analyses are used. Any program-focused management information system suffers from the problem of diffuse and changing program boundaries. This is a significant issue, because deciding which resources, activities, and outputs are appropriately grouped within a program's boundaries will greatly affect the potential outcome of review and evaluation. In any large public agency the proliferation of activities and hierarchical levels can make it difficult to separate programs for analysis (e.g., Warwick, 1975). In addition, many programs become interorganizational in their implementation stage. In a study of state government human service agencies, McClintock (1978) found many examples of programs that were structured to have interorganizational and intergovernmental influences in their planning, budgeting, implementation, and evaluation.

Perhaps a more significant aspect of the boundary problem concerns the definition of program conception or mission. Complications arise when legislative definitions of program are laid over executive agency definitions. In implementing the Budget Review System, many programs that were separate units of analysis with different missions in terms of their authorizing legislation became administratively "comingled" at the agency level. For example, in the area of educational research and demonstration programs, Congress has written separate authorizations for a variety of programs over the years. Some of these legislatively separate programs became grouped in a particular division of the Office of Education and administratively treated as a single program. In the division's requests for proposals, projects that mixed various legislative programs were encouraged for reasons of creativity and efficiency. Difficulties arose when the division received a committee request for budget data on programs that had been comingled in this way for implementation but that originated in separate sections of authorizing acts or even separate laws. The problem is further compounded for a federal level PRES when funds are passed to state and local governments and agencies for implementation and are organized in yet different ways at these levels.

One result of these boundary problems is that no data are reported from administrative agencies on units of analysis that do not conform to the agency's definition of program; or, at best, data are not provided on a timely basis. This means that the operation of PRES must specify priorities for data that are crucial to the budgetary and authorizing processes of the legislature in order to efficiently focus data acquisition efforts.

Defining units of analysis that have operational meaning to legislative and executive groups requires ongoing attention (cf. McClintock et al., forthcoming). In addition to the problems discussed above, program boundaries may change due to new legislation or to the amendment of existing law. The records in PRES would need to reflect changes in authorization in order to preserve an historical perspective on program evolution. Maintaining an updated list of programs that is satisfactory for committee purposes and that does not place undue burden on agency staff is a major task in the operation of a PRES.

PROGRAM DESCRIPTORS

A second matter related to units of analysis concerns the substantive labeling of programs and their activities. An extremely useful capability for the legislative PRES is a flexible on-line review of programs in various speciality areas. For instance, it should be possible to call up data on all programs related to migrant health, developmental disabilities, vocational training, and so on. This requires a program code that is comprehensive, nested in various levels of abstraction, and internally cross-referenced.

In the human services, several taxonomies have been developed that attempt to classify all programs in a defined problem domain and to identify when possible their intended objectives (Human Services Coordination Alliance, 1977; United Way of America, 1976). Ultimately one needs a system that includes text scanning and analysis capabilities such as the bibliographic retrieval systems have, since inquiries about programs may not fall into the categories of a given coding system. In many programs there is wide discretion for implementation by state and local agencies. This means that similar activities may be carried out in programs that are labeled differently. It is necessary to be able to sample programs by type of activity as well as by functional or categorical area.

Also program codes will become outdated as new terminology and activity groupings come into existence. The PRES analyses may proceed by current policy problem issues that cut across program areas. If one wanted to review information on programs related to adolescent pregnancy, for example, it would require the selection of a vast array of human services. This is because in the preventive and ameliorative phases of service provision nearly every functional program area is relevant including health, education, employment, mental health, welfare, and social services (Furstenberg, 1976). The thesaurus guides to computerized bibliographic systems (e.g., ERIC) appear to offer greater flexibility than the service taxonomy codes.

In its initial design, the computerized Budget Review System included the legislative text that defined each program. While additional language might be desirable for purposes of characterizing legislative intent, the textual feature would permit the kind of flexible analysis that would ultimately be desired. A long-term objective for PRES would be a capability of reflecting aspects of implementing regulations, such as program target groups, eligibility criteria, program activities, and geographic characteristics of program sites. Here again one faces the possible disjunction between legislative and executive definitions of program, thus cross-walk procedures are needed that link the structures of each definition system.

Data and Instrumentation

In addition to textual information that describes program intent and activity, there are three fundamental categories of data that can be of use to a legislative PRES—budgetary, evaluability status, and evaluation per se.

BUDGETARY DATA

The Committee on Labor and Human Resources has had data collection experiences with its Budget Review System that are useful to review.

Essentially the committee requested three kinds of budgetary data on each program under its jurisdiction—authorizing amounts, obligations or allocations, and outlays. These data would be needed for the Congressional Budget Process at varying time intervals, in some cases on a quarterly basis, resulting in several data calls to agencies. The formats for recording data evolved from open- to closed-ended questions in order to reduce data processing needs and discretion on the part of respondents. It was not desirable, for example, to permit variation on where or how to allocate management and overhead expenditures or administrative salaries to the outlay figures for legislatively separate but organizationally merged programs. At the very least, one needs to know whether or not the reported data on programs include such administrative amounts and this could be determined with a simple checklist.

The issue of data priorities raised earlier is relevant at this point since, clearly, some information is harder to obtain. For instance, because many federal funds are spent by state and local governments, obtaining timely outlay data is likely to be difficult. Evaluation data, which will be discussed below, may also be problematic since results are rarely clear-cut and subsequent evaluations, secondary analyses, and General Accounting Office reviews may be requested that prolong the period until final assessments can be made (see, e.g., Comptroller General of the United States, 1975).

What is required are standard missing data codes that reflect the variety of circumstances that might legitimately result in no information for certain aspects of a program. For historical purposes these codes should include categories that indicate whether sections of law have been repealed or consolidated. This will allow the legislative analyst to trace the evolution of programs and adapt the specific agency data calls and PRES outputs accordingly.

EVALUABILITY ASSESSMENT DATA

The volume of attention that has been given to problems of program implementation in recent years (e.g., Pressman and Wildavsky, 1973; Bardach, (1977) suggests that it is often inappropriate to gather summative evaluation data at a given stage of the life of a program. It can be helpful, however, to assess a program's evaluability in order to identify problematic areas of program performance (Wholey, 1979). Evaluability assessments are like formative evaluations in the sense that they seek to learn about and sharpen selected program objectives, issues, and processes to the point at which summative evaluation is possible.

Evaluability assessments move through two stages. The first involves a review with policy makers, in this case legislative committees, of their expectations for program performance and for the questions that evaluation data will answer, given the content of authorizing legislation. The second stage involves study of program implementation and identifies those designs, measurements, and analyses that are possible given the way the program has been set up. Evaluability analysis then proceeds iteratively to adjust the features of policy and program implementation to the point at which specific evaluation designs will be feasible and valid.

From the standpoint of the legislative committee, evaluability assessments may be of critical assistance in writing and amending legislation. If it is learned, for example, that there are no stable implementations of the program or that there is inordinate dissension regarding program goals, it may be desirable to have legislative hearings that clarify congressional intent or specify demonstration projects. If there is a disjunction between legislative intent and executive implementation, evaluability assessments will help identify the points of departure and more effective legislature oversight can follow. Often legislative intent is not clear, consists of contradictory objectives, or is driven by the political need to get a bill passed in any form that will work. Stoner's (1977) review of Title I of the Elementary and Secondary Education Act illustrates these states of congressional intent. With Title I the process of writing instructions for program audit procedures finally created an operational definition of legislative intent, which then cleared the way for developing reasonable evaluation strategies.

Standard codes could be developed to reflect need and progress in evaluability assessments. Codes would indicate the extent of program activity, the number of projects started, or the number of persons affected. More detailed progress in the performance of such assessments could be regularly reported by agencies to authorizing committees in order to insure greater accountability in program implementation. Analysis of evaluability data would focus on signals of unusually low activity levels and of uncertainty regarding program goals, plausibility of program models, and intended nature and uses of evaluation data.

EVALUATION DATA

One of the unfortunate aspects of evaluability assessment models (e.g., Wholey, 1979) is that they assume that programs cannot be evaluated until they have clear and consensually validated goals. It is not reasonable to expect all programs to meet a single standard of evaluability. Many human service programs, for example, are faced with endemic uncertainties of technology, political and social environment, and reliable outcome indicators (Hasenfeld and English, 1974). In fact, the patterns of uncertainty that are present in a given program can be helpful in designing appropriate evaluation strategies (Maynard-Moody and McClintock, 1979). This suggests that the nature and the meaning of evaluation data available in PRES may vary considerably. Program behaviors that seem undesirable from a strictly rational goal-oriented point of view may be highly effective in environments of uncertainty (Hedburg, 1979; Weick, 1977).

At a minimum, PRES needs to contain information about what and how many evaluations are under way on a given program and to have provision for early warnings about possible negative effects of programs. More complex data might consist of indicators that showed that some forms of program were robustly effective across sites when others required considerable autonomy to adapt to local conditions. These indicators would be directly relevant to decisions to tighten or relax legislation through amendments. Summary codes could be applied to completed evaluations indicating the results of secondary reviews and the mixture of positive, negative, and uncertain findings. The evaluation reports and related documents could be referenced for more careful examination of details as necessary.

Data Collection

A critical phase of any survey is data collection. While the theory and technology of data collection procedures are steadily advancing (e.g., Dillman, 1978; Bradburn and Subman, 1979), there are many limits to the amount of control that can be exercised. This is due to the fact that data collection normally involves an interpersonal process between researcher and respondent which cannot be as successfully regulated as the logic and mathematics of design, sampling, and analysis. Many sources of random error and bias can be introduced during data collection that will subvert validity in the most elegant and well controlled research and sampling designs. The two major issues confronting data collection for PRES are controlling measurement error and motivating respondents to provide timely and valid data.

As in any survey, a legislative PRES will be more likely to obtain valid data if it can identify ways in which the data or the process of providing data are beneficial to respondents. This is especially important when one recognizes the many layers of bureaucracy that are involved in data collection.

Using the Budget Review System model of the Committee on Labor and Human Resources as an example will help to illustrate how complex the data collection process can become. There are at least four major levels of administrative structure across which the objectives and data of BRS had to pass. These were: (1) the congressional committee and its staff; (2) the top executive levels such as the White House, Office of Management and Budget, and chief policy positions in the agency; (3) the program management level consisting of agency staff who design and monitor program operation; (4) the program operating level at which the activities are performed. If this last level involves grants to state or local governments, then duplicate layers would unfold to double or triple the number of interconnections necessary to produce oversight information.

Even when the number of administrative levels is small, the complexity of the process is maintained by interposing the data collection agent on the picture. In the case of the Budget Review System, the General Accounting Office was the agency responsible for collecting and reporting the desired budgetary information. Given the size of that office and its responsibilities to all committees of Congress, there were at least three levels of staff involved including General Accounting Office policy, supervisory, and program analyst positions.

At each of the administrative and data collection levels there was a possibility for misunderstanding of Budget Review System objectives and for distortion of data. The only solution to the problem was regular interactions among committee staff and personnel from the accounting office and the executive agency program management level, in which objectives and procedures were clarified. In some instances these meetings resulted in revisions of program boundaries (as discussed earlier) or in the modification of data collection instruments and formats. In concept this process was similar to pretesting a survey data collection process; however, the oversight purposes made it more involving and perhaps more threatening than a research study.

Over time the program operating and management levels could report data directly to a legislative office for data processing and computing, and the accounting office or its counterpart in state and local government could engage in spot validation. If desired, the data collection process could pass through a third-party agency since this group could also be responsible for the review of evaluability assessments and agency evaluation reports, much like the General Accounting Office currently functions. There is an important difference between third-party meta-evaluations as a check against misutilization of research findings (Cook and Pollard, 1977) and third-party data collection. Any "field staff" may develop sympathies for the plight of the respondent (i.e., the agencies in this case); and it will require regular review to insure that a professional rapport is maintained between interviewers and respondents (Weiss, 1969).

Analysis and Utilization

The PRES model that has been outlined assumes that certain standard information will be computerized for each unit of analysis that is under review. Most of this information would consist of a textual description of intent and activity and budgetary data with summary codes and references being sufficient for evaluability assessment and evaluation findings. There are three basic legislative functions that can guide analysis and utilization of PRES outputs.

Oversight and control is the most obvious guiding principle. Time series analysis of programs in a given agency and cross-sectional analysis of program types (e.g., health) across several agencies are the most likely strategies. In the latter case, analysis of variance could be used with different agencies as the levels of the independent variable (or agency by functional area, and so on for n-way analyses of variance) and various measures of budgetary, evaluability, and evaluation status as dependent variables.

A second function is the development of legislation based on predictive analysis of future trends. The combination of time series analysis from PRES with special forecasting studies based on econometric data is the likely strategy for committees faced with the need to select an optimal policy. Another analytic need related to the optimal choice problem is to ensure that as many of the alternatives as possible are reviewed. While no one would claim that adequate information is available to truly optimize a choice, by laying out very different alternatives the legislative decision maker can create distinct scenarios which will help sharpen the dimensions of the decision issue. The structure of PRES would permit data on different program options to be arrayed for inspection at a much greater level of detail and speed than is currently possible.

The final analytic function of PRES is to serve as a daily management information system. In this mode PRES could be used to answer basic questions about where resources are going in program areas, which programs are being evaluated, and what client groups in which regions of the country are being served. The number and variety of inquiries from constituents and for day-to-day legislative procedures are limitless. The textual and bibliographic inquiry features of PRES are essential for the flexibility of response that is required for this kind of rapid analysis.

THE LIMITS AND BENEFITS OF PRES IN LEGISLATIVE DECISION MAKING

The process of policy formulation in legislative bodies is intricate in its own ways, involving considerations of cultural, political, burcaucratic, and personal forces that do not easily lend themselves to the technology of social science (Redman, 1973). Obviously, there is no one decision-maker who would interpret PRES analyses and implement changes that were implicit in them. All organizations arc political in the sense that decisions are affected by bargaining and compromise and the legislature epitomizes this process. The complexity, uncertainty, and size of the programs that are under the jurisdiction of most legislative committees make it unlikely that very much coordination and efficiency can be achieved among them.

On the other hand there are adaptive advantages to decentralized and loosely coupled systems that are particularly suited to changing environments (Weick, 1976). For instance, each separate unit (committee or subcommittee) can maintain special environmental sensing devices that are tuned to satisfy needs unique to the unit. Decentralized systems can adapt more quickly since coordination is not necessary, and undesirable adaptations are localized rather than spread throughout the system. There are probably few if any environments that change as rapidly and that highlight constraints as frequently as that of a legislature. In fact, the process of politics in the Congress, as Redman (1973) described it, can be viewed as one of creating or enacting new environments at a rapid pace as the need arises. This means, however, that the possibilities for developing stable patterns of decision making and consistent uses of PRES are problematic.

To suggest that the effectiveness of PRES is limited, however, is not to argue against its utility. There are several ways in which PRES can contribute to the decision making, oversight, and control responsibilities of legislative groups. Most important, it provides back-up support for a management approach that is based on strategic intervention at points of conflict or opportunity. The flexible and comprehensive ways in which data can be arrayed allow the legislator to create alternative views and scenarios in a rapid sequence, which can serve as a compromise mechanism.

There are other benefits of PRES that can ultimately have positive effects on legislative decision making. For instance, by having ownership of its own program data base a legislative committee will be more motivated to ask questions about its own behavior and to sharpen the issues in legislative debate. There is an opportunity for greater direct interdependence among legislative groups and the social science community as PRES analyses suggest a range of special studies or investigations. By reducing the bureaucratic distance between researchers and legislative policy makers, there is likely to be less distortion of information between them and greater mutual ulitization of concepts and data (Etzioni, 1978).

Finally, the use of evaluability data and procedures are likely to encourage approaches to long-range planning and evaluation that are sensitive and responsive to the contexts of programs in the legislative and the executive domains. In this sense especially, the implementation of legislative PRES models should contribute to the coordination among processes of legislative oversight, program evaluation, and improvements in program effectiveness.

NOTES

1. Like Campbell (1975), the present analysis does not assume that social science can or should supplant the social and political processes that have survived through cultural evolution. There is no reason, however, that technical rationality cannot complement political rationality. Allison's (1971) study of executive policy making showed the utility of a variety of perspectives—technocratic, bureaucratic, and political—for enhancing decision-making processes and for explaining how policies are made. It is this viewpoint that best captures the spirit of the present discussion.

2. Many of the observations from which the present analysis was derived were the result of my work as a consultant to the U.S. Senate Committee on Labor and Human Resources from 1976 to 1978. This work was under the direction of Dr. Franklin Zweig who serves as Senior Staff and Counsel to the committee chairman, Senator Harrison A. Williams, Jr. (D-N.J.). To narrow the focus of this analysis, examples will be limited to the federal level. The issues raised are intended to be generalizable to state levels, too.

3. At the appropriation account level, the Committee on Labor and Human Resources has authorization jurisdiction over some 140 programs. By counting programs in terms of specific sections of law, which is desirable from the standpoint of the legislative process, this number jumps to over 1,900. Finally, at the level of implementation in various public and private sector organizations, there are tens of thousands of programs which are the ultimate source of information for program review and evaluation.

4. The Budget Review System was developed as a joint effort of the U.S. Senate Rules and Administration Committee chaired by Senator Howard Cannon (D-NV) and subsequently by Senator Claiborne Pell (D-RI) and the Committee on Labor and Human Resources. Ronald Lee Hicks from the staff of the Rules Committee and Franklin Zweig directed the project with the involvement and assistance of the Senate Computing Center, the Congressional Research Service, and the General Accounting Office.

5. Mr. Stan Jackson of the committee's staff provided the following operational definitions (1) a program is a major activity to implement the mission, mandate, and objectives set forth in the authorizing legislation; (2) an activity is a detailed aspect of a selected program, when such additional detail is useful, comprehensively applied to a program; (3) a project is selected details, aspects or dimensions of a program or an activity that are not comprehensive. It is also possible to aggregate programs to higher levels (e.g., subfunction, function, appropriation account) and to cross-link them with Office of Management and Budget account structures. Therefore, the Budget Review System is capable of meeting committee-specific needs as well as generalizing to related budgetary and evaluation contexts.

REFERENCES

ALLISON, G. T. (1971) Essence of Decision. Boston: Little, Brown.

BARDACH, E. C. (1977) The Implementation Game. Cambridge: MIT Press.

BECKMAN, N. (1977) "Policy analysis for the Congress." Public Administration Rev. 37: 237-244.

BEHN, R. D. (1977) "The false dawn of the sunset laws." Public Interest 49(fall): 103-118.

BRADBURN, N. M. and S. SUDMAN (1979) Improving Interview Method and Questionnaire Design. San Francisco: Jossey-Bass.

BUNKER, D. R. (1978) "Organizing to link social science with public policy making." Public Administration Rev. 38: 223-232.

CAMPBELL, D. T. (1975) "On the conflicts between biological and social evolution and between psychology and moral tradition." Amer. Psychologist 30: 1103-1126.

Comptroller General of the United States (1977) Finding Out How Programs Are Working: Suggestions for Congressional Oversight [PAD-78-3]. Washington, DC: General Accounting Office.

——— (1975) Follow Through: Lessons Learned from Its Evaluation and Need To Improve Its Administration [MWD-75-34]. Washington, DC: General Accounting Office.

COOK, T. D. and D. T. CAMPBELL (1979) Quasi-Experimentation: Design and Analysis Issues for Field Settings. Chicago: Rand McNally.

COOK, T. D. and W. E. POLLARD (1977) "How to recognize and avoid some common problems of mis-utilization of evaluation research findings."

CRANE, E. G., Jr. (1977) Legislative Review of Government Programs: Tools for Accountability. New York: Praeger.

deLEON, P. (1978) "A theory of policy termination," pp. 279-300 in J. V. May and A. B. Wildavsky (eds.) The Policy Cycle. Beverly Hills, CA: Sage.

DILLMAN, D. A. (1978) Mail and Telephone Surveys: The Total Design Method. New York: John Wiley.

ETZIONI, A. (1978) "Linking knowledge to social policy-making: an interview with Amatai Etzioni." Evaluation (special issue): 55-62.

FURSTENBERG, F. F., Jr. (1976) Unplanned Parenthood. The Social Consequences of Teenage Childbearing. New York: Free Press.

HASENFELD, Y. and R. A. ENGLISH (1974) Human Service Organizations. Ann Arbor: University of Michigan Press.

HEDBURG, B. (1979) "How organizations learn and unlearn," in P. C. Nystrom and W. H. Starbuck (eds.) Handbook of Organizational Design (vol. 1). New York: Oxford University Press.

Human Services Coordination Alliance (1977) Services Selection System. Louisville, KY: Author.

KIVENS, L. [ed.] (1978) Evaluation (special issue): 2-30.

MAYNARD-MOODY, S. and C. C. McCLINTOCK (1979) "Organizational analysis and program evaluation research." (unpublished)

McCLINTOCK, C. C. (1978) "Evaluation of human services planning at state and local levels." J. of Human Services Abstracts 3: 26.

—— D. BRANNON and S. MAYNARD-MOODY (forthcoming) "Applying the logic of sample surveys to qualitative case studies: the case cluster method." Administrative Science Q.

PRESSMAN, J. L. and A. B. WILDAVSKY (1973) Implementation. Berkeley: University of California Press.

REDMAN, E. (1973) The Dance of Legislation. New York: Simon and Schuster.

SONQUIST, J. A. and W. C. DUNKELBERG (1977) Survey and opinion research: Procedures for processing and analysis. Englewood Cliffs, NY. Prentice-Hall.

STONER, F. E. (1978) "Federal auditors as regulators: the case of Title I of ESEA," pp. 199-214 in J. V. May and A. B. Wildavsky (eds.) The Policy Cycle. Beverly Hills, CA: Sage.

United Way of America (1976) UWASIS II: A Taxonomy of Social Goals and Human Service Programs. Alexandria, VA: Author.

WARWICK, D. P. (1975) A Theory of Public Bureaucracy. Cambridge, MA: Harvard University Press.

WEBER, M. (1958) "Politics as a vocation," in H. H. Gerth and C. W. Mills (eds.) Max Weber: Essays in Sociology. New York: Oxford University Press.

WEICK, K. E. (1977) "Re-punctuating the problem," pp. 193-225. In P. S. Goodman and J. M. Pennings (eds.) New Perspectives on Organizational Effectiveness. San Francisco: Jossey-Bass.

—— (1976) "Educational organizations as loosely coupled systems." Administrative Science Q. 21: 1-19.

WEISS, C. (1968) "Validity of welfare mothers' interview responses." Public Opinion Q. 32: 622-633.

WHOLEY, J. S. (1979) Evaluation: Promise and Performance. Washington, DC: Urban Institute.

ZWEIG, F. (1979) "The managerial Congress: respectful interfaces between Congress and academia." Presented at Department of Human Service Studies' lecture series on public policy in human services, Cornell University.

Eleanor Chelimsky
The MITRE Corporation
McLean, Virginia

7

EVALUATING BROAD-AIM LARGE-SCALE SOCIAL DEMONSTRATION PROGRAMS

BROAD-AIM, LARGE-SCALE SOCIAL DEMONSTRATION PROGRAMS AND HOW THEY GROW

It seems that broad-aim, large-scale social demonstration programs are always with us, despite the problems they inflict on researchers and evaluators who are charged with the arduous task of examining their impacts, their outcomes, and their processes. Given that these programs originate outside the world of research and analysis, outside the evaluative framework, outside the arena in which we dispute the relative merits of different data sets, for example, it is hardly surprising that these programs should be difficult to evaluate. Their origins lie deep in the worlds of "real"—as opposed to analytical—problems, and of Realpolitik; and the reasons why they develop are multiple.

Social demonstration programs usually come into existence in the first place because a social problem, for one reason or another, has become a major political issue. There then arises a need to respond legislatively and rapidly to public or constituent pressure by means of some relevant, comprehensive (but relatively inexpensive) program which can then be replicated and institutionalized as a service program if it should succeed or relegated to oblivion if it should fail. Social demonstration programs have often appeared to be useful and convenient instruments for filling such a need.

AUTHOR'S NOTE: *This article was presented at the meeting of the Evaluation Research Society of America, November 2, 1978, Washington, D.C.*

As they emerge from the legislative drawing board in the natural course of events, these programs almost always turn out to have very broad aims. Perhaps this is because the problems they address may possess many facets; or because lack of political or social consensus on applicable policy may preclude agreement on more specific aims (see Marris and Rein, 1967); or because knowledge about the causes of the problem is inadequate and it is hoped that a broad general approach may—by chance—provide either a solution, or new information toward a solution, or, at the very least, new information about the problem itself.

Broad-aim social demonstration programs also often tend to be large-scale because it is feared that more modest efforts may be perceived as timorous, "involving too little money spread too thin" (Chelimsky, 1976: 21) and hence unlikely to achieve their political objective which is to placate a particular constituency; or because an agency may have been criticized as a "do-nothing" agency and wants to change that image; or because an agency is new (or is developing a new function) and hopes to prove itself by launching a big, visible program, thereby developing an improved power base.[1]

On top of that, as the program takes shape, the differing demands and needs of policy makers and constituent groups at all levels will then cumulate to even further increase both the number and vagueness of the aims, and the scale of the program, along with the expectations entertained for its success. Additionally, the evolving groundswell for the program will tend to generate a sense of mounting urgency, pushing program developers toward very rapid implementation.

Unfortunately for these programs and for their justification as a useful way of spending tax dollars, the experience of much research and of many evaluations has been that:

(1) When there is not much knowledge about the causes and processes of a social problem, effective program solutions to the problem tend to be hard to find.

(2) Increasing the scope and size of the program solution makes it harder—not easier—to learn something from the effort, either in terms of the problem addressed or in terms of the usefulness of the effort.

(3) The impact of broad-aim large-scale demonstration programs has often been difficult to determine. Many evaluations have ended inconclusively with regard to: (a) whether the program's actual implementation differed from normal or routine operations; and, if so, precisely how; (b) whether the program "worked" in terms of its objectives; and (c) whether any observed changes in the outcome measure could, in fact, be attributed to the program.

(4) The haste with which these programs have typically been generated has been inversely related to the knowledge yield forthcoming from the program's evaluation.

(5) Finally, the broad and multiple aims have tended to weaken the thrust of the program intervention either by channeling resources away from the components most likely to be effective, or because the aims were themselves in conflict with each other;[2] in both cases, there has been a dilution of focus on the social problem being addressed.

Despite all of these failings, however, it does not seem that broad-aim large-scale demonstration programs are going to disappear. The continuing popularity of these programs is assured, in the first place, by the fact that they fulfill many political needs and they do it well:

(1) They can be immediately and appropriately responsive to public pressure.
(2) They can significantly expand many a power base (see Marris and Rein, 1967).
(3) They help new agencies or agencies with new responsibilities to increase their chances for survival (see Downs, 1967).
(4) They are useful in raising consciousness generally and in securing attention, at the local level, to federal objectives, especially in situations in which federal intervention is either difficult or proscribed.[3]
(5) Finally, they are instrumental in buying time during which political or legal issues can be allowed to "ripen" (see Bickel, 1962) while governmental mills grind slowly to some consensus.

Second, these programs may be the best or even the *only* policy instrument available in some cases. (For example, if the Congress presses agencies to move in a particular area and the agencies are restricted to program grants—rather than to changes in tax codes or widespread subsidy programs—then these programs, along with information dissemination systems, are about the only tools available; see Glennan et al., 1977.)

Third, the importance and urgency of a social problem may simply dictate the use of these programs. The push to appropriation is then accompanied by a general hue and cry, a deepening sense of crisis, and statements to the effect that it is high time to stop studying the problem and do something about it.[4]

Fourth, in cases in which approaches other than demonstration programs (approaches such as regulation, or subsidy, or legislative change, or tax incentives, for example) are, in fact, feasible, difficulties as arduous as (or worse than) those of demonstration programs have often occurred.

The inability to achieve balance among conflicting regulations, the equity problems, and uncontrollability which have beset subsidy programs are cases in point. Again, as opposed to these available alternatives, demonstration programs offer the key benefit of reversibility: If they do not work, they can be turned off.

But if one accepts the premise that these programs will likely continue to be authorized whatever the probable effectiveness of their performance, it then becomes essential to pose the question of how we can improve that performance. Now, as discussed earlier, it has been extremely difficult in the past to develop a knowledge base from which to modify these programs because of the problems encountered by the evaluations designed to examine and assess them. Therefore, one logical way in which to improve these programs is to improve our capacity to evaluate them. Well-planned and responsive evaluations can be counted upon to improve program implementation and management and to increase the interest and involvement of program managers and practitioners. This should help to improve program performance in and of itself, but evaluation also brings with it the critical benefit of better knowledge about a program and about the social problem it addresses, as well as a better foundation for constructing alternative solutions.

Although the evaluation of social demonstration programs has posed very difficult problems to researchers in the past, there presently exists a highly favorable climate for new efforts in this area because federal, state, and local policy makers now have a powerful set of political incentives impelling them toward improved evaluation. These incentives are: (1) the increasing competition for funds nationally; (2) the on-going fiscal problems of our cities; and (3) the so-called taxpayer revolt, all of which simultaneously imply a greater requirement that expended public funds be carefully accounted for and increased public attention to agency management, to legislative oversight, and to the budgetary function at federal, state, and local levels. Zero-base budgeting, sunset legislation, the responses to the various incidences of California's Proposition 13 across the country, and the tax bill passed by the 95th Congress are all indications that there is awareness at all governmental levels of a newly and sharply constrained fiscal environment.

ISSUES IN THE EVALUATION OF
DEMONSTRATION PROGRAMS IN GENERAL

Demonstration programs tend to pose problems to evaluators even when they have a narrow focus which is operationally defined. This is because there is a great deal of confusion about what a demonstration program is and what it should do. Everyone seems to have a different definition of "demonstration"; further, those definitions have changed over time.[5] In the early 60s, for example, Herzog wrote that a demonstration program "tests out a hunch or conviction based on experience or practice and *systematically builds up evidence* designed to show whether the hunch or conviction stands up to the test" (italics added; 1962: 212) in a real-world environment. In other words, a demonstration program in 1962 was an experiment which took place outside the laboratory.

Ten years later, however, it seems that a proselytizing goal was added, and Milton wrote that the demonstration program was defined as: "an action planned to *prove* that an innovation is an improvement, with the additional express purpose of convincing others that the innovation should be duplicated" (italics added; 1972: 5). That definition went on to say:

> Demonstrations generally proceed from the belief that the innovation will work. An experiment, on the other hand, proceeds from the identification of a problem and the controlled testing of alternative ways of dealing with it. Demonstrations have evolved because of the need to find new solutions to social problems *without extensive experimentation* [italics added; 1972: 5].

The problem here, of course, is that it is difficult to *prove* improvement in a social problem is extensive experimentation is *not* done. This 1972 definition, then, was somewhat ambiguous and included some inherent contradictions, but it is clear that, in 10 years, the prevailing view of the demonstration program had expanded; in fact, it had doubled. It now included two goals—to prove and to convince—instead of one.

By 1977, Glennan et al. wrote a new definition which stated that a demonstration involves: "an innovation operated at or near full-scale in a realistic environment, for the purpose of: formulating national policy *or* promoting the use of the innovation" (italics added; 1977: 3). That is, demonstrations should seek to do one of two things; *either* they test an idea or innovation to determine its worthiness for inclusion in policy *or* they try to convince people that they should use an already-tested innovation which has not yet been widely diffused or adopted. A demonstration program to *formulate* policy, then, will seek to prove value. A program to *implement* policy will seek to promote use.

From the viewpoint of both the program and of its evaluation, however, the question of definition is of paramount importance, since the program activities, the evaluation design, the objectives to be achieved, and the knowledge to be produced would all be very different, depending upon the kind of demonstration implemented (that is, whether it was intended to test value or to disseminate and transfer what has already been tested).

On the one hand, in the case of a demonstration to *test the value* of a new aid to learning—for example, the objective of the effort might be to find out whether or not students learn more quickly via the innovation than by traditional methods—the activity would need to be quite narrowly focused as is appropriate for a test; the design implied might be some form of the experimental model, along with a process analysis to help explain the outcomes; and the knowledge to be produced would be information pertaining to:

(1) the effectiveness of the innovation in terms of the objective
(2) its acceptability to students, teachers, and parents
(3) its generalizability to other populations
(4) its costs and other operational characteristics
(5) the limitations of the analysis based on the execution of the evaluation design.

On the other hand, in a demonstration to *disseminate or transfer* that learning-aid innovation (once tested and shown to be effective), the objectives might be (1) to increase market penetration and use of the innovation at a wide variety of new sites and (2) to institutionalize (i.e., achieve adoption, adaptation, or integraton) at the test site(s). The activities would, of course, be dictated by the conditions of the original test and by the evaluation findings with regard to the *general* characteristics of the innovation which had been viewed as important in its success. The evaluation design might be an in-depth process analysis examining routine behavior and departures from that routine in various sites. Finally, the knowledge to be produced might include information pertaining to:

(1) the amount of market penetration and use achieved and the factors involved
(2) the amount of institutionalization achieved and the factors involved
(3) comparison of the effectiveness results achieved in the dissemination sites with those of the test sites
(4) indications for the future transfer of this and similar innovations
(5) costs and other operational characteristics of the demonstration
(6) predicted versus actual generalizability
(7) limitations of the analysis

Thus, although various demonstration programs may have elements of both purposes (to test and to disseminate) especially at different points in time, the implied dissimilarities in program activities and in evaluation, and the need of the dissemination effort to build upon the findings of the test, would appear to suggest that a demonstration-test should certainly occur before a demonstration-dissemination. This, however, has not always, or even typically, been the case. On the contrary, evaluation after evaluation has found that programs have proceeded from some untested (or inadequately tested) belief that a particular intervention would be useful, and have then—without further evidence or ado—been implemented and disseminated throughout the country. The kind of decision making which produces these unsubstantiated programs has recently been described as resulting from:

(1) overconfidence by planners, developers, and specialists in theories spun from meager evidence
(2) conviction fueled by a conjunction of some preexisting personal agendas
(3) premature commitment to deciding more than needs to be decided
(4) failure to address uncertainties in such a way as to prepare for reconsideration
(5) insufficient questioning of scientific logic and of implementation prospects (see Neustadt and Fineberg, 1978).

Such decision making derives also, it would seem, from the terrible haste and cauldronlike atmosphere in which federal programs are often generated. Most important, however, it results from the fact that there exists no normal procedure for demonstration programs, in most agencies, whereby interventions are systematically tested and evidence is systematically weighed *before* dissemination can take place.

Even when demonstration-tests *have* been carefully prepared, however, the job of evaluation has not typically been an easy one, especially in social program areas. Before examining the particular problems involved in evaluating broad-aim multisite demonstrations, therefore, it may be useful to look at some issues in the evaluation of a *non*-broad-aim, *non*-multisite social program in an action setting.

ISSUES IN THE EVALUATION OF WELL-SPECIFIED DEMONSTRATION-TESTS IN AN ACTION PROGRAM SETTING

In the case of a well-specified program to test whether a given intervention helps to ameliorate a fairly well-understood social problem (to reduce infant mortality, for example), there is a fairly well-established evaluation planning procedure to follow. The program's objectives can usually be clearly focused (which infant mortality is to be reduced? that is, mortality due to which disease or to what ascribed cause? perinatal mortality or mortality throughout the first year of life? infant mortality among which populations? where? by how much will it be reduced? and so on); so can the program activities (which intervention will be implemented? by whom? for how long? at what cost? and so on); a logical chain of assumptions can be drawn to show why it is reasonable to expect that a certain type of intervention is likely to reduce a certain kind of infant mortality among a certain population, by a certain amount; and it is typically possible, also, to show how this change, if it should occur, can be measured (what data can be collected, what analysis performed, and so on).

When the social problem is less well understood, however—as in the case of crime and criminal behavior, for example—it becomes more difficult to set overall objectives which are meaningful (especially in areas in which not much evaluative research has been done). There may exist few standards of comparison, if any, and it may not be understood how particular activities should, in fact, impact an outcome measure such as crime rates. Often an important function of the evaluation in such cases is to establish, after some period of program operations, what a reasonable objective of the program should be.

Whatever the social problem, however, and whatever the substance of the program intervention, no matter how focused and how well specified the test may be, it is *always* very difficult to apply an evaluation design to an action program. It is true that the problems which affect the development and execution of an evaluation design are very well known (see, e.g., Campbell and Stanley, 1963; Weiss, 1972), too much so to bear exhaustive or extensive recapitulation here. Suffice it to say that the major problems, as they recur in the literature and in the experience of most evaluators, appear to be the following:

(1) the ability to impose an experimental design in an action-program setting (see Guttentag, 1973)
(2) the consequent difficulties of attributing observed changes in the outcome measure to the program and of generalizing beyond the program to other populations
(3) the existence of standards against which to measure outcomes
(4) the availability and "collectability" of data as well as its accuracy and reliability
(5) the cooperativeness of practitioners
(6) the degree of implementation of the program to be evaluated at the local site.

As a means of coping with some of these problems, evaluators have emphasized the importance of evaluative criteria for site selection, to be established while the program is still in the planning stage, as a means of ensuring:

(1) that there are both local need and local interest in the program, as well as the capability to implement it
(2) that the implementation will be sufficient to permit evaluation
(3) that cooperation will be high enouth to get through the difficult phases of the researcher/practitioner interaction
(4) that no insurmountable substantive or procedural obstacles exist which will interfere with the execution of the research design
(5) that local commitments to the evaluation (e.g., data collection, implementation monitoring) will be carried out.

When site selection is carried out in haste, however—as occurs often because of the particular political origins of many demonstration programs —this kind of careful process is slighted and it is not at all unusual to find program components scheduled for "implementation" at sites where state or local law in fact precludes such implementation.[6] By the time the federal agency discovers this, the site has already received its money and it is too late to do much about it.

Even at its best, however—that is, carefully planned and carefully executed, in a program well designed to permit its application—social program evaluation has not always delivered what was expected of it. Findings and procedures have come under attack for many and varied reasons, such as:

(1) the vulnerability of the methodology
(2) the paucity of information derived
(3) the lateness, or untimeliness, of the results
(4) the inability to answer important (but unquantifiable) questions (see Chelimsky, 1977).

A good many of these criticisms may well derive from great expectations, given that:

(1) *all* research designs executed outside the laboratory are methodologically assailable in one way or another
(2) rigorous designs *cannot* accommodate more than one or two research questions, at most
(3) the time-period for executing a formal evaluation may not coincide with the point in time when its results are needed by an agency

(4) the core issues posed by a program may have to be ignored in a rigorous outcome evaluation because they are not susceptible to quantification; thus information may be produced on trivial or peripheral questions which have the key benefit of being "researchable" (i.e., quantifiable; see Chelimsky, 1977).

The question then becomes a problem for researchers. In effect, if formal program evaluation is not adequately responsive to the needs of its sponsors (federal, state, and local agencies as well as the Congress), then, should such evaluation be altered? And if so, how? To this end, many researchers have recently been calling for the development of new strategies for evaluating social programs, among them, process evaluation. During a symposium on the use of evaluation, Crain commented on the need for process evaluation (in conjunction with outcome evaluation) in the following terms:

> What randomization does is tell you that the treatment did indeed have a particular effect, because there is no other explanation except sampling error. However, in the case of ESAP [a U.S. Office of Education funded educational demonstration program], the treatment was nothing but money. Obviously, handing $10,000 to any school in the United States at any time will not cause a rather sharp increase in the achievement tests scores of black male students. We had to then start picking it apart, and figuring out what it was they really did with the money. What were the local conditions that caused it to pay off? And there are some details to the puzzle which don't work out very well. . . . There simply wasn't enough emphasis on trying to figure out what was actually done with that money [1977: 80].

In short, what Crain and others were saying is that there is a major problem in omitting process evaluation, because outcome evaluation, standing alone:

(1) is unhelpful in explaining *which* components of an overall program are the key components
(2) cannot interpret the findings (that is, cannot say how and why they came to be what they are)
(3) usually remains nonprescriptive (that is, the findings tell whether or not the objective has been achieved; they do not ,indicate, and policy makers cannot infer from them, a course of action to be taken in the event of failure).

Thus, while it is true that process evaluation is much more assailable methodologically than outcome evaluation executed according to an experimental design, the argument runs that the experimental design is not suitable for many action programs anyway, that process evaluation using qualitative techniques could address more, and, more important, questions than outcome evaluation, that it would not need to adhere to so rigorous a time schedule, and that it could thus be more responsive and helpful to the evaluation's users.

But given the importance, then, to researchers and to program evaluation sponsors of incorporating process analysis into program evaluation, the question then arises as to why such incorporation typically does not take place. There are many possible reasons which can be advanced (among them lack of time and money) but certainly two major contributing factors should be mentioned here. First, although it is true that some researchers have long recognized the need for systematic process evaluation—it is now 10 years since Weiss and Rein (1970) initially called for "process-oriented" research—no accepted methodology for such research has been developed. A researcher wishing to integrate process analysis into a program evaluation is therefore confronted with the problem of producing an original process methodology, in addition to performing the process research itself.

Second, all evaluators have not always recognized the need for process analysis; and when they have, they may not have done so early enough in the research (as in the example of the ESAP evaluation discussed above) to be able to integrate that effort into the study of outcomes. This problem seems to be linked to the history of the experimental research model which:

(1) tends to foster quantitative rather than qualitative analysis and hence encourages outcome (which is typically quantitative) rather than process (which may be qualitative, descriptive, and difficult to handle analytically)
(2) has been in use for a long time and presents advantages and frailties, both of which are well understood
(3) developed from origins in the laboratory where process (or treatment) was usually simple and well defined, such that extensive analysis of that process was not a requirement (as opposed to social action programs in which treatments are typically complex and cannot be *assumed* to have been implemented as planned).

The need for process analysis thus arises specifically in social action programs in which interventions and institutions are not simple, in which outcomes need to be explained, and in which qualitative analysis, in consequence, is inevitably involved.

Thus, although process evaluation, service delivery assessments, evaluation monitoring, and a host of other process examinations are increasingly being demanded, there is as yet little consensus about appropriate methodologies for the evaluation of social programs via nonexperimental designs. The problem here is that, without consensus among researchers about a process methodology, any evaluation using such a methodology is likely to come under strenuous attack. This can be especially prejudicial and unfortunate in controversial areas in which there is a lack of political and social consensus; it is here that reasearch and evaluation have perhaps their greatest need of credibility.

In sum then, even supposedly simple, well focused, well-specified action programs have not been either very easy to evaluate or has that evaluation always been well appreciated. The evaluation of broad-aim multisite programs, however, is vastly more difficult; and there are many characteristics of these programs which cause this to be the case. Among the many, three characteristics in particular are important to understand: *complexity*, *weakness of specification*, and *weakness of implementation*.

ISSUES IN THE EVALUATION OF BROAD-AIM, LARGE-SCALE SOCIAL DEMONSTRATION PROGRAMS

As Weiss and Rein have defined it:

> The term broad-aim program is intended to describe programs which hope to achieve nonspecific forms of change-for-the-better, and which also, because of their ambition and magnitude, involve unstandardized, large-scale interventions and are evaluated in only a few sites. These characteristics have been shared by a number of social action programs launched during the 1960's—the delinquency prevention and grey area programs, portions of the poverty program, and the Model Cities planning program.[7] These programs attempted to produce increased community competence, increased participation of low-income citizens in community action, and more effective utilization of existing institutions. All these aims could be realized in many alternative ways, and none of these programs could be judged by whether one particular end was achieved [1970: 98].

From the viewpoint of the evaluation, then—given the numbers of interdependent and interrelated aims, the nonspecific improvements to be achieved, and the large size and scope of the interventions to be implemented—the most immediately striking characteristic of these programs is their complexity.

Complexity

As noted above, the objectives of broad-aim, large-scale social demonstration programs are general, vague, and some are even unstated. In a new anticrime program presently being developed by the U.S. Department of Housing and Urban Development (HUD), for example, the three stated objectives are:

(1) to reduce crime in and around public housing
(2) to reduce fear (that is, to improve residents' perceptions of security)
(3) to produce new knowledge about what works in these two areas.

But two unstated objectives, with great importance for the evaluation, also emerge from statements by HUD policy makers, and these are:

(4) to achieve a high degree of participation, by tenants and housing authority people, in decision making about the program, in program activities, and in evaluation activities
(5) to "get the money to the housing projects where it is needed" *as fast as possible.*

The importance of unstated objectives comes from the fact that different objectives within the same program may be in conflict with each other (in whole or in part), and vagueness or omission (i.e., unstatedness) typically hides ideological conflicts or policy ignorance about what needs to be done. In the HUD program, for example, the first objective—to reduce crime—and the third objective—to produce knowledge about "what works"—are conciliable only if there is time in which to do evaluation planning. The fifth (unstated) objective—to start spending money urgently—therefore places the crime-reduction and knowledge objectives in obvious conflict and will jeopardize the achievement of either or both, if the time to set up an appropriate research design cannot be found.

Conflicting objectives in broad-aim social demonstration programs appear to be almost inevitable, however, arising much less from ignorance about their discordance than from the need to conciliate the rival political requirements of social problems. It is in this way that programs to provide health care are expected to ensure quality service to all and at the same time encourage an optimal distribution of scarce medical resources; that welfare programs are expected to provide assistance to those living in poverty and at the same time maintain work incentives (see Rivlin, 1971). Similarly, criminal justice programs are expected to increase crime control and public security and at the same time maintain standards of fairness to individuals and of equality among them before the law. But it is no easy matter to plan programs which can do all of these things. In fact, contradictory or conflicting objectives can make evaluation impossible (as noted above) or can force the evaluator to make choices among objectives. In LEAA's High-Impact Anti-Crime Program, for example, capacity building at the local level conflicted with the federally felt need for rapid action—to the detriment of program achievement (see Chelimsky, 1976). Cities were expected to hire staff, improve their planning and evaluation capabilities sufficiently to implement complex and sophisticated analytical techniques, prepare plans using these techniques, and have projects implemented and operational, "on-the-street," all within six months. Every one of these activities did turn out to be feasible, but only over a much longer term.

The objectives of broad-aim demonstrations are not usually measurable. and it is important to recognize that they would not be measurable even if the program were tightly and admirably constructed, simply because it is not known how to measure them, to "improve health" or "improve the quality of life" are such objectives. In other cases, objectives are not measurable because the data needed for their measurement are not available (because of the confidentiality of criminal records of drug users or juveniles, for example), or do not exist (regional epidemiological profiles, for example). At present, there exists no system which can trace the evolution of a criminal case or the processing of a criminal defendant from arrest through disposition and treatment to the point where the person is returned to society. Yet such a system is a crucial need for the evaluator examining the effects of an offender rehabilitation program. At present some agency records are not even complete enough to allow analysis of offender processing within that agency. But even if the records *were* complete, accurate, and reliable, they still would not allow the examination of questions requiring a knowledge of offender processing across the criminal justice system as a whole. At present, it is thus very difficult to measure the outcomes of court processing changes, to examine system effects (e.g., the impact of an intervention in one agency on another agency further down the line in case processing), or to study the recidivist outcomes of the various diversion, probation, rehabilitation, or incarceration programs implemented in a given locality or region.

A final aspect of complexity worth mentioning here is that local autonomy and the ability to develop action projects freely according to local needs—which are highly desirable things from both policy and effectiveness viewpoints—come into conflict with the needs of the evaluator, who wants a uniform treatment and wants to standardize projects (or units of projects) so as to be able to compare activities and outcomes across those projects. Also, when there are many sites, each doing its own thing, it is very rare indeed that program activities and data collection can be monitored adequately.

In sum, then, a major problem for the evaluation of broad-aim programs is their social and ideological complexity which have general, unstated, conflicting, unmeasurable, and even unachievable goals. The particular difficulty posed here to evaluation is that logical links cannot then be established between the legislation, the program objectives, the allocated resources, the program activities, and the program outcomes that would allow a research design to be meaningful applied to that program.

Weakness of Specification

Another characteristic of broad-aim, large-scale demonstrations is their weakness of specification. There is a lack of clarity about what will be done, who will do it, how it will be accomplished, and why it is reasonable to expect that a particular activity will help to achieve the goal targeted. In many cases, uncertainty at the federal level is due to a desire to be flexible, to allow local sites freedom to develop or choose program components. In others, however, it is due to confusion.

The Impact Cities, Model Cities, and Pilot Cities demonstration programs all tried to disseminate quite complicated ideas which had not yet been tested, which involved quite vague and unclear activities, and which *could not* be tested in the turbulent settings in which the programs evolved.

In the HUD program presently being developed, the same confusion is manifest. Does the agency seek to demonstrate something which is known to be effective and which it would like to see picked up and adopted in many public housing projects around the country? No, because there is admittedly little research knowledge that any of the concepts being proposed is effective in reducing crime. Is the agency setting out to test whether these concepts do in fact reduce crime? No, because the program would then have to be a carefully controlled test; and rigorous evaluation designs are inappropriate, as we have seen, for broad-aim large-scale programs. Moreover, urgency to "get the money to the housing projects where it is needed" is such that even the most ordinary evaluation planning to produce at least *some* good information appears to be problematic. The program, then, is a demonstration but no one knows what is being demonstrated.

Another problem which commonly besets large demonstrations is the specification of federal, state, local, and research roles in the program. Who will do what? How will review and approval of program activities occur and at what levels? How will start-up and implementation delays (which affect the evaluation) be handled? It should be noted that ambiguities attached to the role of the states in the anti-crime programs of the eight Impact Cities were responsible for major program delays. In all large demonstrations, however, imprecision about the roles and responsibilities of the different levels of government gives rise to frictions which focus sometimes on planning issues, sometimes on people, but may well be based—in reality—on the question of political control of a federal program.

Weakness of Implementation

Finally—and this will come as a surprise to no one—there is, almost always, weakness of implementation. In a federal program implemented at the local level, typically there are uneven starts and inadequate thrusts. There is federal uncertainty of local need largely because programs are generated in such haste that local need can never be clearly ascertained. In many cases, there may in fact be a perception of local need at the federal level which is only partially shared at the implementation site. Some programs may be philosophically unpalatable to some local implementors. (In the Improved Lower Court Case Handling Program, for example, the pretrial release of arrestees on their own recognizance presented major problems of acceptability to criminal justice system people in South Carolina.) There may be a lack of administrative or bureaucratic incentives likely to inspire motivation or zeal among implementing personnel. There may be interference by various levels of bureaucrats who have been (or feel they have been) bypassed; there may be inadequate skills, accompanied by even more inadequate technical assistance, and inevitably there is differential project and personnel attrition. (Many two-year demonstration projects may, in fact, really be only one-year efforts, because project staff spend the second year looking for new jobs.) As Williams has written about the problems of implementation:

> In the case of a major program in a large social agency, the multitude of layers and actors involved in the implementation process is striking, perhaps even appalling. With so many complex layers of power and authority, it is easy to lose the sense of direction that steers one toward the basic goals of the organization. What could be more obvious and fundamental than the fact

that decisions need to be implemented, and that inattention to implementation will almost certainly be fatal? Yet a fantastic amount of bureaucratic foliage so obscures the way that social agencies can lose sight of this. Responsibility for implementation tends to slip between the cracks. Almost everyone assumes that specification and implementation are somebody else's task. Higher-ups see implementation as being a lower-level responsibility; but the lower levels look to higher echelons for specification and guidance. . . . No one denies the importance of implementation, yet everyone has reasons why their office cannot or should not undertake it. When implementation responsibilities ever do get picked up, it is usually by a lower-echelon unit which cannot avoid them [1975: 549].

In some demonstrations, when implementation *has* been achieved, the local version may bear no resemblance at all to the federal demonstration program. This, of course, may be related to the weakness of program specification described above, but in any case it presents special problems to the evaluator. Once federal funds have been disbursed, however, it is difficult if not impossible to affect implementation from the federal or state level, short of a careful monitoring system. Such a system, of course, cannot be improvised but must be planned in advance of implementation, and separate funding should be envisaged; otherwise, monitoring monies may well be sacrificed toward other functions which appear to local decision makers to be more urgently needed. At best, however, such a system should not be expected to "cure" the problems of implementation. What it will do—and this is not negligible—is to provide early warning of implementation problems to upper management and to potential evaluators, as well as furnish an account of implementation activities which may, later on, be able to help in explaining project outcomes.

During the national evaluation of LEAA's High-Impact Anti-Crime program, implementation problems in eight Impact Cities were so acute as to retard program operations by more than a year. Most important among the problems reported by the various city projects were staffing difficulties and inordinately lengthy administrative review procedures occurring within the intergovernmental environment.

In accordance with these findings, which appear to be common among large demonstration programs, it is often said that implementation is essentially a bureaucratic or political problem. In another sense, however, it is a research problem as well. As discussed earlier, one of the reasons why process analysis is needed and is usually lacking is that the complex implementation of a real-world environment can never be *assumed* to have occurred (as one might assume, for example, the existence and process of such implementation in the laboratory). The study of implementation processes, therefore, has typically been given short shrift by researchers and these processes—especially as they concern demonstration programs —remain poorly understood. This is unfortunate since the appropriateness of an evaluation design can only be determined with regard to the implementational and organizational contexts in which it will be executed.

Essentially, both weakness of specification and weakness of implementation affect the evaluation of program impact by affecting program operations: It is, of course, difficult to evaluate a program which does not exist, or which is only partially implemented. Yet the history of social demonstrations continues to be afflicted with such programs and such evaluations.

In summary, then, there exists a rather formidable array of problems which vitiate or hamper the evaluation of broad-aim, large-scale social demonstration programs. Some of these problems will clearly require a great deal more research before possible solutions can even begin to be formulated. In other areas, however, efforts to address certain of these problems can and should be undertaken, given:

(1) the likelihood that these programs will continue to be funded
(2) the need of the Congress and government agencies to obtain useful information from them
(3) the public requirement to improve their performance by making them more effective and more efficient.

SUGGESTIONS FOR IMPROVEMENT

What, then, are the areas which may be accessible to treatment and change in the evaluation of social demonstration programs? It appears from the above discussion that there may well be some actions which can be taken—by the Congress, by federal, state, and local agencies, and by researchers—to reduce some of the problems currently encountered. Toward this end, some suggestions are offered here as a means for improving our current ability to evaluate, and learn from, demonstration programs.

Size of the Program and Purpose of the Analysis

Although it hardly seems likely that the broad-aim aspect of demonstration programs will be negotiable (given that they arise as the result of the ever-present political forces discussed earlier), federal agencies should render these programs more evaluable:

(1) by distinguishing between demonstration-tests and demonstration-disseminations
(2) by implementing the smallest possible number of demonstrations which seek *both* to test and to convince
(3) by sharply restricting the scale of implementation, when the effort is intended to assess an untested (or incompletely tested) concept.

Time to Plan the Research

Perhaps the most important program dimension which should be targeted for attack in the effort to improve the evaluative performance in these programs is that of *time*. Time is needed in order to perform simultaneous program and evaluation planning adequately.

The Congress and federal agencies should establish that evaluation planning must accompany program planning (with which it needs to develop interactively), and that it must take place before beginning program implementation. It is evaluation planning which can allow improvement of the weakness of specification identified earlier as a typical problem of social demonstrations. It is evaluation planning, again, which comes to grips with broad program objectives (in terms of the strategy and activities set up by program planners) and specifies the evaluation design, the methodology, the measures, the data collection, and analysis procedures. In short, evaluation planning is the basic foundation for assembling evidence to support the subsequent inferences which will need to be made about linkages between program activities and outcomes.

At present, evaluation planning takes place too late or does not take place at all. There is almost never enough time. So that while it is true that the climate in which broad-aim social demonstrations are generated is hardly an ideal one for evaluation planning, more time and effort in this area would allow such planning:

(1) to establish, guide, and communicate the overall design
(2) to facilitate the study of outcome and process by conciliating certain operational or administrative features of the program with the evaluation (as needed)
(3) to try to compensate for or parry some of the other knotty problems posed by broad-aim social demonstrations.

Evaluation planning is not a panacea, however, and will not (for example) allow the execution of an experimental design in an operational setting in which it cannot be accommodated. But such planning, very carefully performed, does allow a much superior yield of knowledge than that which has traditionally been available.

Careful Development of Site Selection Criteria

Federal agencies should make certain that site selection criteria are developed during the period of program and evaluation planning, taking into account not only the requirements of the program per se (which are reflected in criteria like real interest, capability and need at the local level, lack of statutory or other prohibition to the program or its components, population size, geographical distribution, and so on) but also the requirements of the evaluation (e.g., practitioner cooperation, data availability).

Clarity about Program Specifications

Agencies should pay a great deal of attention to the communications they issue about the program, press releases, guidelines, and so on. In all social action programs, it is important to establish and communicate very clearly to program participants information about:

(1) what the program concept is, what kind of demonstration is envisaged, what it is expected to achieve
(2) how much money is available, under what conditions, to which eligible populations
(3) how long the program is expected to be in operation and what plans have been made for its institutionalization
(4) what the federal, state, local, and research roles and activities will be and who, exactly, will do what, exactly
(5) what the program menu will be, what degree of freedom the local sites will have in choosing projects, and whether components of projects can be the unit of choice
(6) how beneficiary/agency/research views and findings will be sought and channeled back to improve program operations
(7) the technical assistance schedule (who is eligible, who performs it, for how long, at what points in the program, and so on)
(8) implementation guidelines
(9) information about the evaluation.

Emphasis on Incentives

Evaluations often appear threatening to agency people and practitioners; cooperation with the requirements of the evaluation is often enhanced if evaluators can offer something of value to program people, or if special funding can be allocated to compensate for extra work caused by the evaluation, for example. Evaluators and/or agencies should try to ensure:

(1) rapid feedback of evaluative analyses to the sites
(2) arrangements for data collection through administrative incentives
(3) separate funding for data collection (at present, when there has been a failure of data collection at the local level, that fact is typically not discovered until the evaluation is due—usually long after the program is over; funding for data collected would be available only after completion of the effort)
(4) separate funding for implementation and evaluation monitoring (resources need to be allocated specifically for this function, because at present, even in federally funded projects, evaluators do not usually have the resources to fulfill this function and it typically is not performed; without it, however, evaluation and operational problems which could seriously affect the information yield from the project will go unflagged and unaddressed).

A Mix of Evaluative Strategies

Some evaluation is always needed for major demonstrations, even if it only takes the form of an audit, of monitoring, or of service delivery assessment. Evaluation should be external to and independent from project operations, but should include planned input from   and *feedback to*—practitioners, agencies, and beneficiaries. It is possible in some demonstrations to have an overall evaluation plan which includes different multiple-site designs: some simple pre-post designs, some service delivery assessments, and some process evaluations. Agencies should decide *very* carefully which projects should get which evaluations, based on priorities assigned to the evaluation questions which need to be asked. As discussed earlier in the article, however, more work is needed in the development of nonexperimental methodologies.

Technical Assistance

Depending on the type of demonstrations, technical assistance can be very important in the success of the implementation (and hence, in that of the evaluation as well). Agencies should allocate generous funding to this area. Even more important than the moneys allocated, however, are *the manner* and *the schedule*. Too often, high-priced consultants fly in at the beginning of a project, tell the project management, "You need a consultant," and then fly out again. Technical assistance needs to be scheduled throughout the life of a project at particular points, depending on the kind of project it is.

Longer and Later Evaluations

Evaluations are often funded over too short a period for effects to be observed. This may be because of the inherent nature of the intervention (freedom from drug or alcohol use, recidivism, or the effects of job training or vocational education, for example; all need to be assessed over the long term) or because certain types of innovations take a long time to be accepted or are hard to implement, and early evaluations cannot take their measure in any real or useful way. In short, some efforts can be judged in a year, and others cannot. The life of the evaluation should be extended sufficiently to allow the measurement of important effects in a reasonable way.

It goes without saying that these eight suggestions, even if heeded and perfectly fulfilled, will not suddenly procure optimal demonstration programs. They should, however, produce major improvements over what presently exists.

It is now 10 years since Moynihan wrote:

> Wishing so many things so, we all too readily come to think them not only possible, which very likely they are, but also near at hand, which is seldom the case. We constantly underestimate difficulties, overpromise results, and avoid any evidence of incompatibility and conflict, thus repeatedly creating the conditions of failure out of a desperate desire for success [1969: xii].

Perhaps the time has now arrived when we can become less extravagant in our expectations, less hurried in our assumptions, more willing to proceed step-by-step, and more serious about assembling facts, examining the experience of others, and expressing clearly what it is we want to do. Perhaps, indeed, the time has come, but then again, perhaps it has not. Maybe being extravagant and overambitious is an American quality as well as a defect and maybe we should not try to change that, or blush for it. Defensiveness and fear of making mistakes may be more productive of immobilism than of new knowledge. So while we are remembering Moynihan, it may also be well not to forget Toynbee's remark that "the most likely way to reach a goal is to be aiming not at that goal itself but at some more ambitious goal behind it." One thing is sure, however. We should stop promulgating large-scale demonstration programs without having first developed convincing evidence that they will work.

NOTES

1. Gregg noted that power within the bureaucracy derives more from size than from program effectiveness and that there is "greater interest in federal agencies in obtaining and spending larger budgets than in getting results" (1977: 105).

2. For example, the need to learn, to gain knowledge, from a program is almost always in conflict with the need to respond quickly, to "get the money to the people who really need it." And since it is probably the latter need which gave rise to the program in the first place, haste typically precludes the development of an adequate research design, or even the development of an awareness of past mistakes (much less their avoidance).

3. Head Start is an example (Follow-Through is another) of a federal demonstration program developed to decrease educational disadvantage among minority groups, an area in which federal intervention was indicated because of state and/or local failure to act.

4. Mayor Cervantes of St. Louis, Missouri, announcing the Impact Cities Program in 1972.

5. Not only have they changed over time, however, it may also be worth noting that there is a trend in those definitions which seems to parallel the changing *Zeitgeist* of the 60s and 70s, running from hopeful and confident in the early 60s, to grandiose and somewhat fuzzy in the early 70s, to analytical, cautious, and maybe a little sour today.

6. This occurred in the Improved Lower Court Case Handling Program (an LEAA demonstration) in which Columbia, South Carolina, was statutorily prohibited from implementing the police citation and court summons components of the program and in Las Vegas (Clark County), Nevada, where the program's misdemeanant probation component was prevented by state law.

7. LEAA's High-Impact Anti-Crime Program is an example of a demonstration of the 70s which can also be counted among those broad-aim large-scale efforts (see Chelimsky, 1976).

REFERENCES

BICKEL, A. (1962) The Least Dangerous Branch. New York: Harcourt Brace Jovanovich.

CAMPBELL, D. T. and J. C. STANLEY (1963) Experimental and Quasi-Experimental Designs for Research. Skokie, IL: Rand McNally.

CHELIMSKY, E. (1977) In The Proceedings of a Symposium on the Use of Evaluation by Federal Agencies (MITRE Report M77-39). McLean, VA: MITRE.

—— (1976) The National Evaluation of the High-Impact Anti-Crime Program (MITRE Report MTR-7148). McLean, VA: MITRE.

CRAIN, R. (1977) In Proceedings of a Symposium on the Use of Evaluation by Federal Agencies (M77-39). McLean, VA: MITRE.

DOWNS, A. (1967) Inside Bureaucracy. Boston: Little, Brown.

GLENNAN, T. K., W. F. HEDERMAN, L. L. JOHNSON, and R. A. RETTIG (1977) The Role of Demonstrations in Federal R & D Policy (Rand Working Note 10014-OTA). Santa Monica, CA: Rand.

GREGG, J.M.H. (1977) In Proceedings of a Symposium on the Use of Evaluation by Federal Agencies (M77-39). McLean, VA: MITRE.

GUTTENTAG, M. (1973) "Special characteristics of social intervention programs: evaluation of social intervention June 22."

HERZOG, E. (1962) "Research demonstrations and common sense." Child Welfare.

MARRIS, P. and M. REIN (1967) Dilemmas of Social Reform. Chicago: AVC.

MILTON, C. (1972) Demonstration Projects as a Strategy for Change. Dublin, CA: Police Press.

MOYNIHAN, D. P. (1969) Maximum Feasible Misunderstanding. New York: Macmillan.

NEUSTADT, R. E. and H. FINEBERG (1978) The Swine Flu Affair: Decision-Making on a Slippery Slope. Washington, DC: Government Printing Office.

RIVLIN, A. (1971) "Why can't we get things done?" Washington *Post* (July).

WEISS, C. H. (1972) Evaluation Research. Englewood Cliffs, NJ: Prentice-Hall.

WEISS, R. S. and M. REIN (1970) "The evaluation of broad-aim programs: experimental design, its difficulties, and an alternative." Administrative Sci. Q. 15: 97-109.

WILLIAMS, W. (1975) "Implementation analysis and assessment." Policy Analysis 1(3).

Franklin M. Zweig

U.S. Senate Committee on Labor
and Human Resources
State University of New York at Buffalo

8

THE EVALUATION WORLDVIEW
OF CONGRESSIONAL STAFF

Every setting is characterized by unique factors which influence the performance of employees. The Congress and legislatures in general possess some unusual and some exaggerated features which condition staff perception of evaluative research and thus influence its deployment (Froman, 1967; Cummings, 1976). As evaluation personnel become familiar with the special norms and legislative imperatives inherent in the legislative setting, it is likely that evaluation studies will become more useful in assisting public policy making (Weiss, 1973). As evaluation personnel become familiar with the evaluation worldview of congressional staff, it is likely that provider-client relationships will become more productive. This could lead to improved utilization and heightened respect for evaluative research in legislative settings.

The theme of this article is that one must understand the information scanning and trading functions within the conflict-laden flow of events comprising the policy-making process in order to best relate to congressional staff as clients of evaluation personnel. The balance of these comments describes such functions and events and presents hypothetical entry points for evaluative research in that framework. Congressional staff perceptions of "good evaluation" and "bad evaluation" are ventured in the course of describing two forms of legislative policy making, the reauthorization bill and nonroutine or elective legislation. Drawn mostly from my experience, I hope that this article will stimulate systematic research to prove or disprove the themes, variations, and dynamics observed and set forth herein.

STAFF AND INFORMATION:
SCANNING, TRADING, AND COALITIONS

Elected representatives are the decision makers of the legislative process and their staff serve as advisers, information filters, agents, and evaluators. Evaluation in this context is more in the nature of assessment since few staff have been trained in the formal design, implementation, or interpretation of evaluative research. Assessment usually concerns weighing alternatives with the best information at hand and the communication of the analysis to employing elected officials.

The extent to which such assessments are credited depends partly upon the trust existing between the elected official and his staff and partly upon the accuracy, care, and vigor employed in amassing the information fundamental to the assessment. Trust is frequently a product of tested loyalties between the elected representative and his or her staff. It is essential for such trust to emerge and that emergence is predicated upon the demonstrated advocacy of the staffer on behalf of his or her employer. Advocacy is performed in a legal context: continuous staff representation of the client-employer's interests. All assessments are made by staff within this general principle. Congressional staff, unlike many bureaucrats, professionals, and academics, serve strictly at the pleasure of their employers, an individual Congressman or Senator. That service will be terminated when the staff abridge the advocacy principle.

When choices press upon their principals, staff act as agents to gather information. The information scanning and filtering functions are so prominent that some writers (Malbin and Scully, 1977) and the popular press (Cameron, 1979) have suggested that congressional staff are an invisible and unelected legislature. More serious students (Fox, 1977) and my own experience run counter to that suggestion. As a Senate committee staff member for several years, I can attest to the important intermediary performance of staff in the policy-making process, but most staff are careful not to take the boss's place or to inordinately assume that authority has been delegated to them implicitly. To the contrary, most staff members shun being perceived as "getting out in front" of their employers and take great care to check every step which has an overtone of authority.

To be sure, some congressional staff develop protected areas of expertise and others are more highly influential by virtue of tenure, great trust, or proximity to congressional leaders. Infrequently, some staff seek power and achieve it. The typical staff member, however, views his or her job as enormously preoccupied with information predigestion and subsequent transmission to his or her employer to the most unbiased extent possible within the loyalty imperative. Taken together, these elements configure for staff an information scanning role. Since evaluative research is one special kind of information utilized in public policy making, it is incorporated with increasing frequency into the information scanning role.

Information is not only scanned but it is also traded among congressional staff as goods may be traded in any marketplace. In some respects, staff make an information market and the trade on that market is brisk.

Imagine, for example, the irritated reaction of an evaluation researcher visiting a congressional staff person only to be interrupted constantly by telephone calls which the staffer accepts and initiates. Such interruptions are common when Congress is in session and to the trained observer it should soon become apparent that the nexus of telephone contacts available to congressional staff constitutes a most valued "property," the heart of the staff information trade, and the spine of a partially structured exchange which facilitates the trading efforts.

The exchange regulating information is a valued network mechanism similar to exchanges established for transactions of securities or wheat. This "staff information exchange" operates according to a complex, latent set of unwritten rules—prompt return, reciprocal credit cumulation, and future options, among them. The prompt return rule, for example, obligates staff to respond to calls with rapidity unusual in many non-legislative professional settings. The reciprocal credit cumulation rule assures the initiation of calls from other staff who are aware of a colleague's interest in a subject or happening. Both rules work together to build options for future information. Whether these specific rules stand the close scrutiny of subsequent systematic research remains to be seen. Even casual observation, however, will disclose a regularity, patterning, and rational purpose for information practices which may appear excessively intense to persons outside the congressional staff milieu.

Specific rules aside, the pragmatics of the staff information exchange require continuous use of the available network. Events can move with dazzling speed in the legislative arena, and the energies of most staff are devoted in a significant way to avoidance of surprise. Unless the exchange is used regularly, users may be perceived as having dropped out of the network. In such instances, staff cannot function to maintain critical information supply, avoid surprise, and transmit to their employers current status reports and alternative assessments. Face-to-face contacts maintain the network along with telephone contacts, but visits are time consuming and meetings are used mainly to finalize agreements among a group of staff persons, the terms of which were reached in prior conversations.[1]

An information exchange operates outside of Congress among the associations and interest groups established to lobby and influence the course and content of legislation. Such a "lobbyist's information exchange" makes energetic attempts to articulate with the congressional staff information exchange. In bringing the articulation into action, the information transaction between the two exchanges tends to be asymmetrical; the lobbyists tend to supply information and congressional staff tend to consume it.[2]

The concurrent operation and articulation of the two exchanges tend to create conditions conducive to coalition formulation with respect to a given issue or piece of legislation. Transactions within and between the two networks permit all actors to determine the positions of all others in preliminary fashion. Once such measure is taken, the stage is set for recommendations by congressional staff to their employing elected officials. Direct communication between principals is very much facilitated by the information foundation laid in the course of staff utilization of the exchanges.

The sheer volume of information accumulated by congressional staff provides depth for the production of assessments of alternatives conveyed to Members of Congress. These assessments aid the Members in taking positions on bill introduction, cosponsorship of legislation introduced by other Members, voting on bills in committee or in the congressional chamber, and public postures on various issues treated in the policy-making process.

THE POLICY-MAKING PROCESS
THE CONTEXT FOR
STAFF INFORMATION FUNCTIONS

Several writers have described the policy-making process as an incremental flow of authoritative decisions institutionalized in government and created in a climate of continuing partial conflict (Lindblom, 1968; Dror, 1968; Dye, 1978). This analysis of the process embraces as well the position advanced by Banfield (1961). In Banfield's conception the policy-making process is instituted to satisfy the needs of various interest groups which in successive episodes make proposals for change in public policy in order to advance their own private interests under claim of enhancing the public interest.

For evaluators, it may be useful as well to view the policy-making process in part as congressional staff experience it: a clash of morally armored constituencies over claims to the content of the law or the benefits of the public purse. A morally armored constituency is usually an association, organization, or coalition sharing strong beliefs about a provision or direction of public policy. Over time, these beliefs are codified into missions and lexicons. They forge a foundation for positions of groups and organizations linked by issues as the incremental flow of policy-making moves ahead in time.

Clashes among constituencies are initiated when an interest group or coalition presents its wishes or demands to a legislature, a court, or an executive agency. These policy-making bodies have the legitimacy and authority to transform such proposals into binding and enduring decisions. Such decisions will benefit some and cost others, and will be promoted and resisted accordingly.

The policy-making process is at base an adversary process. Competing interests attempt to influence policy makers and to sway the decisions of Members of Congress. Congressional staff frequently are the first recipients of information provided as an initial step to convince decision makers of the merits of a given proposal.

Conceptually, each surging and conflict-laden episode in this process can be outlined roughly into four stages, each of which activates congressional staff information functions and each of which has salience for evaluative research.

The Proposal Advanced Stage

An interest group, alone or in coalition with others, advances a proposal for changes in law or expenditures of public money. This proposal is presented in terms of its alleged advantages to the public, but it will in most cases be found to result in significant advantages for the proposing interest group. The proposal is disseminated, quietly at first lest it prematurely stimulate opposition. As time passes and the proposal is fortified, the proposing interest group or coalition disseminates the proposal widely, and frequently enlists mass media in order to create broad awareness of the proposal among policymakers and the public.

A coalition is formed to rally numerous organizations and interest groups behind the proposal if one did not formerly exist. The purpose of the coalition is to expand the proposer's potentials for influencing policy makers to favor the proposal. If previously formed, the coalition is broadened or strengthened through recruitment of new participants. In creating coalitions for proposals of major proportions, every attempt is made to recruit as many organizations as possible in order to rally the widest possible array of "publics" behind the proposal.

Counterproposal Advanced Stage

An opposition forms in response to the intial proposal, above. An opposing interest group is activated by the perception that the initial proposal presents a threat to its vital interests. Coalition formation is likely to follow to support this opposition if such a coalition had not previously existed. The opposition has three basic alternatives in service of its interests:

(1) defeat the offending proposal with finality
(2) modify the offending proposal to make it more acceptable to the opposition
(3) introduce a counterproposal as a substitute for the offending proposal and work to have it adopted by the legislature as a law or appropriation of funds using the same methods of interpersonal influence and media campaigns available to the proposers.

Conflict Stage

The activation of an opposition precipitates a period of conflict in which proposers and opposers utilize some or all of the political, economic, and technical tools at their disposal to achieve results favorable to them. The ensuing period of conflict may be characterized by various degrees of adversariness depending upon the interests and benefits at stake, the actors involved, and frequently, serendipitous or vexatious unanticipated forces. Thus, the conflict stage may be expressed as friendly competititveness, vigorous contest, or vituperative attack and rancorous counterattack. A conflict episode can manifest all of these expressions and countless others as well.

Conflict Resolution Stage

Whatever the form or intensity of the conflict, resolution of the controversy is the function of the Congress (and of all legislatures). Once an issue is ripe for legislative action, an authoritative determination of the policy or the expenditure is made by law or numerous other legislative devices.[3] Only a limited number of general resolutions is possible, however, and the universe of outcomes includes the following:

(1) The proposers win—the proposal is enacted or adopted largely as advanced.

(2) The opposers win—the proposal is defeated or substituted with a counterproposal.

(3) A compromise is reached—the most frequent outcome, by means of which all parties receive some benefit from the adoption of a modified proposal, a modified counterproposal, or a merged form of proposal and counterproposal.

(4) The controversy is deferred—the contending proposals are temporarily removed from the congressional agenda to reduce the heat of conflict or to permit a cooling off period out of the public limelight during which compromises may be reached.

(5) The proposal is permanently removed from the agenda—at least for the foreseeable future of a congressional term—in order to prevent the intensity of the conflict from exceeding limits causing the legislative process to lose control over the issues, the parties, and the forum.

Once completed, the process comes to rest, if only briefly. The resolution reached in a given cycle of policy making sets the stage for the next cycle. Cyclical repetitions create policy increments.

STAFF COMMUNICATION IN THE POLICY-MAKING PROCESS

Their information scanning and trading functions permit congressional staff to keep under close scrutiny the unfolding stages of the policy making process. The staff information exchange is exquisitely sensitive to interest groups, proposals and counterproposals, coalitions, nature of the conflict episodes, and possibilities for conflict resolution.

Monitoring the policy-making process is extremely important to the Congressman or Senator. He or she undertakes first-hand monitoring and relies on staff for corroboration and additional information. The Congress interfaces with interest groups whose interests span the nation and whose proposals and counterproposals potentially trigger the state constituencies of every Senator and the district constituencies of every Representative.

If caught unaware by some issue in the policy-making process, the elected official can be misled and inadvertently may take positions in a controversy which later may be regretted. The staff information function reduces the possibilities of such error and enhances possibilities of building a rationale for the Congressperson's position in the controversy. In this way, the staff information function in the policy-making process enhances rational decision making.

When their bosses are partisans in the policy-making process and favor a proposal or counterproposal, staff are affected by that position and frequently find that their access to information exchanges becomes limited accordingly. To the extent that the elected official does not take an early position favoring one or another proposal, his or her options are preserved and the staff member is free to use the maximum network capability of both exchanges as a "neutral" information scanner and trader.

Whether a restricted or free information exchange is available to the staff member, evaluative research is one of the kinds of information traded. It is a form generally valued for its "objective" character, its ability to focus issues, and its ability to rationalize arguments in the adversary process. Since two kinds of policy-making—regular reauthorization and nonroutine legislation—are encountered in legislation, the salience for evaluation in each type is worth considering.

SALIENCE OF EVALUATIVE RESEARCH IN
REAUTHORIZATION BILLS

When legislation expires and must be reauthorized periodically, the termination schedule itself creates the time intervals for beginning and ending each cyclical loop, that is, sequence of stages, of the policy-making process.

For example, the Elementary and Secondary Education Act of 1965 is the federal government's major education assistance program to states and local education agencies. It is funded at approximately $6 billion a year, half of which is used to provide compensatory education for poverty-stricken children. It is authorized in five-year cycles. The timing of the policy-making process with respect to this act is thus built directly into the legislation. While it is possible to change authorization dates by means of subsequent legislation, Congress gears its consideration of the issues covered in this act to the five-year reauthorization schedule. Since many controversial issues are included, such as aid to desegregating communities, it is understandable that Congress resists opening them up for action in less than the mandated five-year reauthorization periods.

In recent years, evaluative research has held special salience for regularly reauthorized legislation. Using the congressionally-mandated study as its instrumentality, elected officials have built unanswered questions directly into law and required answers to those questions by means of a program of evaluative research. Frequently, special appropriations of funds have been designated to carry out this evaluation effort. Such studies and inquiries mandated by Congress have depended in large part upon the formative and summative research methods common to evaluation.

In 1974, for example, the Congress mandated a massive study of the effectiveness of the federally funded compensatory education program. At stake was a fundamental policy decision whether to allocate federal funds according to poverty levels or according to educational test scores, a decision which would shift concentrations of local funds drastically. A $15 million appropriation was made available for the conduct of this evaluation by the National Institute of Education (NIE, 1977). Staff generally were well disposed to this study as were the Congresspersons who authorized it. When reported prior to the expiration of the Elementary and Secondary Education Act in 1977, this evaluation effort was greeted enthusiastically. It was felt to be a successful undertaking and was characterized by the following features:

(1) The policy-relevant questions were posed at the outset of the study in the legislation.
(2) The study was designed as a multiple-component, integrated enterprise with the lead agency, the National Institute of Education, the coordinator of a great many contractors of special analyses and evaluations.
(3) Continuing consultation with congressional staff was built into the study's schedule.
(4) Interim and final reports were geared to legislative events in the reauthorization cycle.
(5) Reports were written in language everyone could understand.

These features contributed to a congressionally mandated evaluation study widely regarded as a success. Such studies can be seen to facilitate the incremental sequence of the policy-making process in two fundamental ways.

First, legislatively required studies add data to the legislative process by means of law. When so enacted, results of the study are made salient by prior congressional commitment to review them. In essence, a promise is made to look at the issue seriously. The review of the data emanating from that promise falls initially to congressional staff in the course of their information scanning and trading routines. Staff conveyance of conclusions, alternatives, and factors covered in the evaluation effort assists position making and position taking by the legislator who will be confronted by various proposals and counterproposals in the reauthorization process.

Second, congressionally mandated studies sometimes are employed to defer conflict otherwise not resolvable in any given policy-making sequence. The delay incurred by "sending a matter to study" thus may unblock a serious obstacle to timely completion of work on reauthorization measures. Whatever subsequent action may occur on the burning issue threatening to block reauthorization can be taken with the help of data and rationalized in a research report disseminated widely. Evaluation data and reports thus provide a focus for dialogue among proposers and opposers party to the issue and may provide avenues to compromise. The time required by the study may also prove soothing.

EVALUATIVE RESEARCH AND NONROUTINE OR ELECTIVE POLICY MAKING

Nonroutine policy making is the process attending legislation any time that existing law does not prescribe scheduling for new legislation, amendments, and changes in direction. In such situations, proposals are offered by interest groups or coalitions at the time calculated to be most opportune. Nonroutine legislative events are subjects for the congressional staff information exchange. As the policy-making process moves from proposal advance to conflict resolution stages, evaluative research attains currency as a tool in the adversary proceedings.

There are many possible tactical uses of evaluative research at each stage of the nonroutine policy-making process. The four lists below are hypothetical pending the findings of systematic inquiry.

The possible actions in the proposal advanced stage are as follows:

(1) prior evaluation results cited as justification for the proposal
(2) evaluation research underway cited as evidence of importance of the public and private interests at stake
(3) results of evaluation studies cited as inducements for supporting organizations to join the supporting coalition
(4) efforts undertaken to certify and elaborate evaluative research project findings through review by selected experts and conduct of various meetings and conferences

(5) favorable evaluative research incorporated into lobbying materials and procedures

(6) syntheses of evaluative studies attempted in order to create a sense of consensus and comparability among supposedly disinterested experts and investigators when that consensus is favorable to the proposal

(7) steps taken to anticipate attacks upon the credibility of the evaluative research cited.

The possible actions in the counterproposal advanced stage are as follows:

(1) prior evaluation results cited as justification for the counterproposal

(2) evaluation research underway cited as evidence of importance of the public and private interests at stake

(3) results of evaluation studies cited as inducements for supporting organizations to join the opposing coalition

(4) efforts undertaken to certify and elaborate evaluative research project findings through review by selected experts and conduct of various meetings and conferences

(5) favorable evaluative research incorporated into lobbying materials and procedures

(6) syntheses of evaluative studies attempted in order to create a sense of consensus and comparability among supposedly disinterested experts and investigators when that consensus is favorable to the counterproposal

(7) attempts made to discredit the evaluative research utilized by interest group or coalition advancing initial proposal and steps taken to protect evaluative research from attack by those opposed to the counterproposal.

The possible actions in the conflict stage are as follows:

(1) attacks upon credibility of the parties' evaluative research sharpened, disseminated, and made public

(2) search for a second, corroborating level of evaluative research documentation conducted and analogous research findings sought

(3) attempts made to strengthen weak areas of evaluative research cited in the exchange of attacks.

The possible actions in the conflict resolution stage are as follows:

(1) if the process ends in compromise, a mandate to evaluate the outcome is likely to be forthcoming.

(2) if the process ends in a clear victory for the proposers, the evaluation studies utilized in the process by the proposers are likely to be institutionalized as an authoritative base for future studies

(3) if the process ends in a clear victory for the counterproposers, the evaluation studies utilized in the process by the counterproposers are likely to be institutionalized as an authoritative base for future studies

(4) if the controversy is resolved by removing it from the public policy-making forum, evaluation studies may be prescribed as a means to negotiate differences prior to return of the controversy to the legislative agenda.

STAFF COMPLAINTS ABOUT EVALUATIVE RESEARCH

In both reauthorization and nonroutine legislation, congressional staff encounter difficulties in utilizing evaluation. Conditioned by their information scanning and trading functions within the policy-making process, staff voice some common complaints about evaluative research. While not exhaustive, the following complaints and suggested remedies are heard frequently.

First, the weaknesses of a given study often are not apparent until subjected to the close review made by opponents in the adversary process. Reliance upon a study may thus entrap a staff member into a position with respect to a proposal. Training in evaluation may help, but a number of staff have suggested requiring forthright statements of study limitations at the outset of a report in bold type. In short, one avenue for improvement may be to require product labeling, a "truth in evaluation reporting" concept.

Second, congressional staff express concern that professional standards available as reference points for practice of law and economics are not operable in the evaluation field. The absence of codes guiding professional evaluation practice appears to reduce staff confidence in evaluation products. Many staff suggest the adoption and publication of such codes and standards as a condition for contracting participation in congressionally mandated studies.

Third, even when evaluators are careful to relate study objectives to policy issues (too infrequently the case according to many congressional staff), comparability among highly focused evaluation studies is so rare that congressional staff are faced with immense difficulties in relating studies at their margins. Until evaluations utilize policy analysis literature searches in designing evaluative research, this issue will not be remedied. Until the organizations funding, publishing, and disseminating evaluation reports aggregate studies by problem or policy issue and conduct secondary analyses linking studies within aggregated clusters, a foundation for creating comparability will not emerge. Until bureaucracies funding evaluative research require comparability with antecedent or concurrent studies in some form, the license to evaluate will not be channeled into a policy-functional literature.

SUMMARY

The evaluation worldview of congressional staff is predicated upon and largely shaped by the need to give and receive information in the course of their service to their client, elected officials. Systematic evaluative research holds promise as a useful feedback device to assist staff work. Evaluation in legislation in all likelihood will become more central to the worldview of congressional staff as the legislative branch requires more information for policy making. Recent successful experience with congressionally mandated evaluation studies seems to have reinforced the utility of evaluative research for staff members dealing with the Elementary and Secondary Education Act. Evaluation is a tool in the adversary milieu inherent in the policy-making process and congressional staff frequently voice suggestions for its improvement. Evaluators who are familiar with that milieu are likely to improve their services to their congressional clients.

NOTES

1. Informal meetings occur, of course, and support information exchange. Formal meetings feature the staff mark-up, among others. The staff mark-up includes staff representatives of legislators having a stake in a bill, a provisional draft of which is negotiated for presentation to the legislators. Staff go over a bill and attempt to achieve consensus about its provisions. Staff mark-up results are communicated to the legislators who then take positions which they represent at committee meetings during the actual, as opposed to staff, mark-up of the bill.

2. The executive agencies—i.e., the so-called bureaucracy—constitute a third exchange. Sometimes the appointed and civil service officers employed by the executive branch constitute a special lobby. More frequently, the executive branch operates as the third party in transactions involving the Congress, the administration, and the interest group community. For the illustrative purposes of this chapter, only the congressional staff and interest group exchanges are described, although the administration plays an important and unique role in virtually every area of public policy making.

3. A law authorizing governmental activity in the form of a program or enforcement action is a common legislative device. A resolution expressing the sense or preferences of one or both houses of Congress is another commonly employed legislative device. Appropriations acts allocate resources. The publication of agreements or understandings in the *Congressional Record* is a less authoritative but frequently desirable legislative device to accommodate multiple interests and resolve conflict among those parties.

REFERENCES

BANFIELD, E. C. (1961) Political Influence. New York: Macmillan.

CUMMINGS, F. (1976) Capitol Hill Manual. Washington, DC: Bureau of National Affairs.

DROR, Y. (1968) Public Policy Making Reexamianed. San Francisco: Chandler.

DYE, T. (1978) Understanding Public Policy. Englewood Cliffs, NJ: Prentice-Hall.

CAMERON, J. (1979) "The shadow Congress the public doesn't know." Fortune (Jan. 15): 38-46.

FOX, H. W. (1977) Congressional Staffs: The Invisible Force in American Law Making. New York: Macmillan.

FROMAN, L. A. (1967) The Congressional Process: Strategies, Rules, and Procedures. Boston: Little, Brown.

LINDBLOM, C. E. (1968) The Policy Making Process. Englewood Cliffs, NJ: Prentice-Hall.

MALBIN, M. J. and M. A. SCULLY (1977) "Our unelected representatives." Public Interest 47: 16-48.

U.S. National Institute of Education (1977) Compensatory Education Services. Washington, D.C.: Department of Health, Education and Welfare.

WEISS, C. (1973) "Where politics and evaluation meet." Evaluation 1(3): 37-45.

ABOUT THE CONTRIBUTORS

Eleanor Chelimsky has been associated with The MITRE Corporation since 1970. She directs planning and policy analysis there and heads MITRE's criminal justice, program evaluation, and research management work. She is currently developing an analysis of demonstration program processes and issues debated at MITRE's recent symposium on federal program institutionalization.

Joseph F. Coates is a Senior Associate with the Offices of Technology Assessment of the U.S. Congress. He also holds adjunct positions at George Washington University and American University in Washington, D.C. His major professional interest is in planning for the future. The impacts of technology on society is one of his principal concerns.

Joseph Comtois has been a group director in the General Accounting Office for nine years. He has served in that capacity in the Office of Policy and Special Studies, the Financial and General Management Studies Division, and the Program Analysis Division. His experience includes the application of systems analysis in reviews of all types and leadership in developing program evaluation activities. Mr. Comtois has a BS from University of Connecticut and was a graduate fellow in systems analysis at MIT.

Ronald Lee Hicks is a senior analyst on the staff of the U.S. Senate Committee on Rules and Administration. Previously, he was with the U.S. Treasury Department in a variety of positions, in the U.S. Customs Service, and a program analyst in the office of the Secretary of the Treasury.

Keith E. Marvin has been an Associate Director in the General Accounting Office for 12 years. He has served in that capacity in the Office of Policy and Special Studies, the Financial and General Management Studies Division, and the Program Analysis Division. His experience includes the applications of systems analysis in GAO reviews of all types and leadership in developing program evaluation activities in the GAO. Mr. Marvin has a BA from Doane College and BS in electrical engineering from Iowa State University.

Charles C. McClintock is an Assistant Professor in the Department of Human Service Studies in the College of Human Ecology, Cornell University. He has directed several regional and national evaluations of human service delivery and planning systems and served as a consultant to the U.S. Senate Committee on Labor and Human Resources and various local, state, and federal agencies. His research interests include methodological issues in survey research and program evaluation. His current research focuses on the effects of uncertainty on organizational learning and innovation. McClintock received his Ph.D. in Psychology from the State University of New York at Buffalo where he also served as Field Director for the Survey Research Center.

Hillel Weinberg is legislative assistant to Congressman Benjamin A. Gilman of New York. Weinberg was previously legislative assistant to Congressman Don Young of Alaska and has also served as staff assistant to the House Commission on Administrative Review, consultant to the Senate Committee on Human Resources, and instructor in the U.S. Department of Agriculture Graduate School. He currently resides in Arlington, Virginia.

Carlotta Joyner Young is completing her Ph.D. on utilization of evaluation in the Department of Psychology, Pennsylvania State University. She has evaluated numerous local and state level educational programs. In 1978, she served as an analyst with the U.S. General Accounting Office.

Franklin M. Zweig (Ph.D., Florence Heller School, Brandeis University; J.D., State University of New York) is a legislative counsel on the chairman's staff of the U.S. Senate Committee on Labor and Human Resources. He is also a Professor of social policy and planning at the State University of New York at Buffalo.